Editing In Brief

Editing In Brief

Gene Gilmore
University of Illinois

Robert Root
Eisenhower College

The Glendessary Press · Berkeley

Preface

Training a capable newspaper editor is a long and challenging task. Even the best editors can recite their flaws and shortcomings. They know they need to deepen their knowledge, to polish familiar skills and develop new ones, and to adapt to the swiftly changing world they help report.

Five chapters on editing can provide only the fundamentals needed by a beginning editor, but these chapters give the journalism student a start toward being a competent editor. The workbook section can help the beginning editor develop his skill because the stories there are filled with errors, and the first job of an editor is to find mistakes. The second job is to correct them. Dozens of other steps need to be taken to produce quality work.

The five chapters of this book are taken directly from *Modern Newspaper Editing,* by Robert Root, who died in 1970, and myself. The other fourteen chapters in the parent book cover makeup, news crises, law, ethics, policy, research, the work of the various sub-editors, and the future of newspaper editing. The student who is stimulated by editing and aspires to a career in journalism will want to read those chapters. Then he will want to get a job on a newspaper that prides itself on editing and continue his learning there. Once he has his basic knowledge, his future depends upon his talent, personal ambition, and opportunities.

The student should realize that he must master fundamentals first. He needs to spot and smooth awkward sentences. He needs to find misused words and correct them. The student who leaps over these basic skills may find his professional life restricted.

Anyone entering news work should realize that print journalism is undergoing great technological change. The finished product does not look much different from what it did a generation ago. But inside the news room and the printing plant there are astounding new machines that can set type at lightning speeds, instantly recall stories on a cathode ray screen, and make pictures into engravings in a few minutes. Many more changes are coming. The serious journalism student should at least know about them and be ready to master them when he can.

This book provides the basic information and techniques which the student editor, like the athlete or musician, can learn and practice. Admittedly, practice can be tedious and exhausting, whether in learning tennis or piano. But after a while practice makes the skill a little easier and more satisfying. The student who finishes this work book with satisfaction is on his way to becoming a good copyeditor.

G. G.

Acknowledgments

A dozen or more persons and organizations helped in the preparation of this book. Most of them, but not all, gave help as the parent book, *Modern Newspaper Editing,* was prepared. Thanks go to Dr. D. Wayne Rowland, dean of the School of Journalism, Drake University; Professors Edmund C. Arnold and Roland E. Wolseley of the School of Journalism, Syracuse University; and Professors Glenn G. Hanson, John Schacht, Lynn Slovonsky, and W. William Alfeld of the University of Illinois College of Communications.

Help came from these professional journalists: Charles Puffenbarger of the *Washington Post;* Charles-Gene McDaniel, science writer of the Chicago bureau of the Associated Press; Larry Hale of the *Binghamton* (N. Y.) *Press;* Gerald Bean of the *Rockford* (Ill.) *Register-Republic;* and Vincent S. Jones, former executive editor of the Gannett newspapers and past president of the American Society of Newspaper Editors.

Special thanks go to United Press International and Associated Press for permission to use altered versions of their stories.

The editors of *Editor & Publisher, Quill,* and *Journalism Quarterly* deserve a note of appreciation for the many articles printed on newspaper editing. They have been valuable in preparing the book.

Most important, however, was C. H. Gustafson of Glendessary Press, who suggested this book and edited the manuscript.

Contents

1 The copyeditor and copyediting

Newspaper copyeditors have a special place in the newsroom. On the bigger papers they sit at a horseshoe-shaped table, the copydesk, encompassed by paste pots, pencils, scissors, copypaper, and one another. On smaller papers their center is more likely to be a group of flat-topped desks, pushed together so the copyeditors can work efficiently as a team.

The copyeditor's job, of course, is to edit manuscript, or copy. This job, sometimes called simply "editing," is to remove words, alter language, and trim away surplus stories or parts of stories until the finished newspaper product is concise, accurate, factual—and appealing. To be a good judge of copy, the editor needs to combine his interest in the English language with an understanding of reporting, some knowledge of printing processes, and a clear understanding of his own newspaper's policy.

The path of copy

The substance of his work is copy—the reporter's manuscript (usually double-spaced on cheap copypaper), which comes to the editor from three main sub-editors.* The city editor sends copy from his city reporters. The state editor provides stories about events from the paper's circulation area outside the city. The telegraph editor delivers copy selected from the wire services. Some papers even have a fourth sub-editor, a suburban editor, who transmits news and features from the suburbs.

The person in charge of the copydesk is the *slot man*, so called because he sits on the inside—in the slot—of the horseshoe desk or its equivalent. His aides, the copyeditors, sit on the outside and so are known as *rim men*, even though occasionally two or three of them will be women. (Copyeditors are also called *desk men* and *copyreaders*.) Figure 1-1 shows a typical arrangement.

* The term "sub-editor" is descriptive but not much used in U. S. newsrooms. In Britain, however, "sub-editor" is common professional usage.

The slot man selects the rim man best able to handle a particular story. He also decides how it should be edited, then writes a curt phrase like "trim," "cut," or "slash" above the story. The slot man may be still more specific. He may write "trim one-third" or may even jot down the number of inches the story should measure when set in type. The copyeditor then understands he must reduce the story to exactly that length. A copyeditor also has some of this executive power. He may cut a story more sharply than ordered or even kill it, but he will probably want to discuss his reasons with the slot man. Others have already planned space for his copy and must know how many column-inches he has trimmed.

Sometimes the slot man will suggest a certain handling of a story. He may write cryptically "Trim out the puffs" or "Bring fire angle to top." But all orders from the slot are not written. Since he is only feet away from his rim men, the man in the slot may shove a story across with "Sharpen up that lead on this stuff of O'Hara's—it's too long. And move it along, ahead of that Latin story."

The notations by the slot man include a symbol to tell the copyeditor what size headline to give the story. It may be simply "C" or "E" or "2/36." Any one of these may mean "two columns of 36-point tempo heavy italic type." The editor knows the shorthand of his paper and can write the head accordingly. (Headlines are discussed more fully in chapter 4.)

Fig. 1-1. Copydesk. The copydesk of the **Binghamton (N.Y.) Press** (circulation 78,000) has six copyeditors working under the direction of the slot man. The news editor, standing, normally sits behind the slot man on the rim so he can be in easy communication with the desk chief. The room in the background contains the wire service teleprinters.

This editorial teamwork occurs at a single desk on medium and large newspapers. All local, state, and wire copy crosses this desk. Because stories from all three sources come from everywhere, the desk is called "universal." Only sports and women's news usually are edited at separate desks.

A few metropolitan newspapers receive too much news to use the universal desk system. They divide the flow of news into "city," "national," and "world" operations. Local, suburban, and state copy comes to the city desk, and all wire news and stories from special correspondents go to the world desk. But in this system sports and women still remain worlds apart.

Small newspapers, of course, do not use enough copy to keep a full desk busy, so each sub-editor himself edits the appropriate stories from reporters or wire services. For example, the "city editor" may edit the copy written by one or two local reporters and himself, including sports stories, while a "telegraph editor" may handle international, national, and state news from the wire, as well as copy from correspondents in nearby villages. There then has to be an informal system of consultation so sub-editors know how much copy is flowing and what the top stories are.

No matter how simple or complex the system, an editor must concentrate on improving copy. He tightens, points up, trims, polishes. But he should *not* make over stories by altering every one so it will read as though he wrote it. Reporters seethe when clever phrases are made prosaic or novel leads are made routine. The editor should apply his pencil with care, for he should encourage originality. The best newswriting is sprightly and varied. An editor who makes all copy read alike mechanizes writing; and as Dean Danielson of the University of Texas observed (after working with computers in news research), "If you write like a machine, you can be replaced by a machine."

**The nature
of desk work**

The special qualifications of a copyeditor bring him advantages. In most cases the pay is better. American Newspaper Guild contracts usually set the base pay of editors at least five dollars above the minimum salary for reporters. Since copyeditors are in demand these days, salaries sometimes are pushed above Guild scale and frequently well above the minimums.

The way to promotion most often is by way of the rim man's chair. As copyeditors usually have been reporters, the combination of reporting and desk experience makes a newsman valuable for positions requiring more than one point of view. The first step for a copyeditor usually is over the desk into the slot. But he may be boosted directly from the rim to such jobs as state editor, city editor, suburban editor, telegraph editor, or picture editor. His first promotion may even be to assistant city editor or assistant state editor. These jobs then prepare him to move up to the more responsible and best-paid positions as editor, assistant to the publisher, executive editor, news editor, or even editor-in-chief.

Even at the beginning, in the informal atmosphere of the copy desk, the copyreader is in good company. Most desks are populated by bright men and women with superior wit and humor who appreciate a well-turned phrase. Copydesk wisecracks are told all over the newsroom, and from time to time they show up, without attribution, in a local column. Most of the joking is done during the lulls that occur during the work day, for copy tends to come in spurts. After working at a good pace for an hour or so, an editor can take a few minutes to relax. During these breaks editors often spoof each other, rib the copy boys, or even comment on the boss's foibles. Satirical pokes at local, state, and national stuffed shirts may start a serious discussion of world affairs.

If a young newsman enjoys being up-to-date on current affairs and ideas, he will find the copydesk in the midst of the news flow.* On the small paper editors tend to be better informed on the full range of human events than anyone else in the community and thus have a special responsibility to stay up-to-date. On the large paper the desk man can become expert on a few specialties. Like the professor, he amasses knowledge on a favorite subject or two; but, unlike the professor, he is not pressed to delve for the minutiae and to publish. His scholarship is an avocation. But desk men have written books on their pet subjects and received the acclaim of scholars, and substantial royalties as well.

Though it provides great rewards, copyediting also includes some frustrations. Editing is sedentary, and the lack of physical activity bothers some people.† Egos also get little exercise, since the work is anonymous. The reporter can get a byline, but no one ever sees a story topped "Headline by Joe Guggenheimer." The copyeditor's fame rarely extends beyond the newsroom, so he has to be satisfied in large part by his belief in doing an important job well. Editors find their egos strengthened most by the approving chuckles or praise from their associates or, best of all, from their bosses.

The man who enjoys being out where the news is made and hobnobbing as a reporter with the big names may miss the excitement when he is brought in to the desk. Though writing headlines and reshaping stories has its creative possibilities, the copyeditor who is at heart a writer may be unhappy without the creative challenge of writing news and feature stories. Not all newsmen are cut out for this relatively unspectacular side of the editorial operation.

Perhaps the greatest and most surprising drawback in desk work

---

*Copydesks once were the preserve of older staff members. Now, because there are more jobs than seasoned staffers, young men and women often are put on the desk right out of journalism school.

† The sedentary aspect of desk work would be no disadvantage for some handicapped persons. Dick Thornburg, editor, *Cincinnati* (Ohio) *Post* and *Times-Star,* has noted that "copyediting offers a useful and reasonably well-paid career for young people— men and women—who are crippled in body, but not in mind or spirit or ambition. ... A person who showed special talents in newspapering could readily become a city editor or a managing editor, even though handicapped."

is inactivity. While breaks can be stimulating, long slack periods can be depressing. This is particularly true on the biggest newspapers, where there are several editions and the staffs are large enough to cope with almost any emergency. By hard work the first two editions are taken care of, and subsequent editions rarely require many changes. There may be almost nothing to do for an hour or more, yet the editor can't count the time as his own. If a slack period comes at the end of the work day, most slot men let a few copyeditors go home half an hour early. If a rim man can spend his slack times reading magazines or books, he will turn a disadvantage into an advantage. He "gets his reading done" on company time, and the paper gains from his widened knowledge.

Much of the negative side of copyediting can be eliminated by real appreciation from the deskman's editors and colleagues, a good principle for the copyeditor who moves up the hierarchy to recall. Praise when the copyreader has made a complex story readable or turned out an exceptional headline is worth almost as much to him as a raise in pay.

The *St. Petersburg* (Fla.) *Times* underlined the value of accurate editing with a game of "killing enemy errors." "X-act Agent" buttons were distributed to 664 staffers, along with special blue pencils. The paper paid $25 to the one who circled the most errors. Perhaps a corny gimmick, but it showed every reporter and copyeditor that management cared about quality.

Reporters who appreciate the efforts of editors boost the morale of the desk, as an example at the *New York Times* illustrates. A member of the *Times'* Washington bureau wrote a letter to the city room expressing appreciation for checking doubtful points with him. To the amazement of deskmen, a breed accustomed to too little praise, he wrote: "I read my story this morning with just the greatest pleasure, noting where, as always, you had smoothed some lumpy sentences, chopped apart some overly long ones, skillfully made a couple of internal cuts in exactly the right places and, in short, made the story better than the one I had written."

The alert professional

Whether working on small or large papers, editors have to keep tabs on themselves, for they can go stale on the job. A man who develops professional skill remains, it is hoped, a credit to his profession. But a lazy newsman can drift through several years, unaware of changes in newspapers, oblivious to undercurrents in world affairs, and unwilling to prepare himself for more demanding tasks. He goes nowhere.

The editor with the brightest future is a reader. He reads magazines and the best newspapers, and at least skims through the current books, while thoroughly reading some of the old ones. His reading alerts him to change and to ideas. News almost by definition concerns itself with change and ideas, and an editor unfamiliar or uninterested in them becomes ineffective. He will gain neither the responsibility nor the respect of a professional.

Even a competent editor can slip unconsciously into getting careless about the fine points of his job. He may allow slips in grammar because he has let slide the occasional few minutes necessary for review. A well-thumbed book on grammar shows that an editor is concerned with details of quality—and therefore probably concerned with quality in general.

A good desk man can obtain tips for quality writing and editing in three or four minutes of reading every day or so. One of the best sources is *Winners & Sinners*, "a bulletin of second guessing issued occasionally from the southeast corner of the *New York Times* News Room." This one-sheet paper recounts the journalistic blunders and triumphs of Timesmen. The *Cleveland Press* publishes a similar paper called *Tips and Slips*, and a medium-sized paper, the *Wilmington* (Del.) *Journal-News*, turns out *Hits & Misses*. These sheets help greatly in preventing editing mistakes. Books like Strunk and White's *Elements of Style* and Gowers' *Plain Words, Their ABC* (see Bibliography) prod the editor to make sure that his copy uses words correctly and that the language is simple and direct.

The copyeditor takes aim

The goal of the copyreader is to be sure that the stories in the paper are in good, readable, accurate English. He looks at the message and structure of the whole story. But he also fixes all its minute parts. For example, he catches dangling participles. One paper ran a photo of a lost child, with this sentence in the cutline: "Wearing only a diaper and rubber pants, police guessed his age at 12 to 14 months." The copyeditor should have seen that the police were more appropriately dressed.

He also blocks mixed metaphors, such as this quadruple one from a paper submitted by a journalism student: "This then is the key. The potential is pushing at the dam's gates. Given the proper catalyst, we may be on the threshold of witnessing an entire new era of journalism." With luck, maybe the key will keep the flood from getting through the door.

Verne English, long a copyeditor for Syracuse newspapers, kept a file of writers' boners the desk had caught. Here are samples, the kinds of things that the sharp deskman spots:

—Four juvenile boys admitted the theft.
—Dear licenses outsold marriage licenses.
—Passengers were treated to a mid morning concert shortly after noon.
—The General Electric Advanced Electronics Laboratory shot its last employee Saturday as the company's flu vaccination program ended.
—A post-mortem autopsy was performed.
—The hospital reported she was pregnant but the injuries did not effect it.

Copyediting shorthand

A visitor to a newspaper newsroom is often surprised that the paper ever comes out. "How can you keep everything straight?" "Aren't there all kinds of problems that take hours to solve?"

The answer, of course, is that all the jobs mesh. The result is a newspaper with nearly all the words spelled correctly, the main news events reported, all the space filled with a good blend of news, pictures, commentary, and advertising.

One of the reasons so much work can be done in such a short time is that, except in slack times, no one on a newspaper staff spends much time in conversation. On many papers the top editors spend a half an hour a day in conference deciding how the main news of the day will be played. But the rest of the work is a routine with almost no conversation during busy periods. Each man does his job quietly.

That picture may surprise those who imagine the newsroom filled with people screaming orders at one another. Actually the noise level is not much higher than in a bank. The reason for the lack of noise and conversation is that newsmen have a silent language.

The headline order, as mentioned before, comes to the copyeditor in the form of a written symbol. The slot man marks the copy with a string of other cryptic orders, like *kill, add, more,* and *jump.* Other symbols are little more than a scratch of a pencil. The editor uses all this sign language on copy so that the printers will know, without being told orally, what he wants done. The signs he puts on stories are understood in every composing room in the country. The editor uses these symbols unconsciously, just as a touch-typist punches typewriter keys without thinking where his fingers should go.

the symbols used ~~common~~ in every newsroom in the

country may see puzzling to the student at

first, but a few hours practice removes their Mystery.

*Symbols
in editing*

Start new paragraph:

Jones said he arrived at 10 a. m. Rogers insisted that

the time was 10:45.

Set in lower case instead of capital:

The Biology class met outdoors.

Capitalize:

Los Angeles--President Nixon signed the tax bill.

The supreme court will hear the case at noon.

The supreme court will hear the case at noon.

Insert and delete:

He profesed a belief in ghosts and the conshseus of opinion was that he was sincer.

Insert new word:

The bookkeeper allegedly spent the money at the races.

Separate elements:

Everything had been all right that morning.

Transpose elements:

Alabama

He only won two games.

Close:

He started as a copy reader and worked his way up.

Close, but leave space:

The fourth is freedom of   the press.

Connect elements:

He said that he saw the three men enter the building and that the men were injured.

Insert period:

The U.S. team won the match.

The U.S. team won the match.

Insert comma:

The tour will include Ireland, Scotland and Wales.

Insert colon:

Prizes were awarded in three categories fiction,
nonfiction and poetry.

Insert semicolon:

The winners were John McIntyre, for fiction Paul
Barnes, for nonfiction and William Ellis, for poetry.

Insert apostrophe:

The reporters story was praised.

Insert quotation marks:

The Golden Pheasant is a musical.

Insert exclamation point:

"Oklahoma" was a hit musical.

Insert hyphen:

Police claimed the thief was caught rehanded.

Insert dash (and exaggerate its length or frame it with short lines):

The bill passed 94 to 2 is the first of its kind.

Abbreviate:

Governor Otto Kerner signed the bill.

Spell out:

Wm. B. Zarfoss won the election.

Use figure instead of word:

The group represented twelve states.

Spell out figure:

He had 1,000,000 counterfeit dollars.

(Spelled out it would be one million.)

Let it stand as first written:

He pleaded not guilty. *stet*

Indent to left:

(The World Almanac gave the figure as 2.25 million.)

Indent to right:

(The Statistical Abstract of the U. S. listed the number as 28.)

Indent both right and left:

(The Denver Post reported that the lost men were rescued within hours of the disaster.)

Center:

Three Kick Goals

Let capital stand (for marking all-capital copy from Western Union or a news service):

WASHINGTON--SEN. HIRAM FONG, R-HAWAII, INSISTED ON THE CHANGE, AND HE WAS SUPPORTED BY THE UTAH DELEGATION.

Change from tabular to paragraph style:

The decision will give these grants to the following states:

Wisconsin, $14 million;

Utah, $7.4 million; and

South Dakota, $11 million

(Long tabulations require no more than one to two of these connecting lines. Mark the margin "Run In.")

Wisconsin, $14 million;

Run in

Utah, $7.4 million;

South Dakota, $11 million;

Ohio, $22 million; and

Kentucky, $14.9 million

Let copy stand as written (if the typesetter may think the copy is mistaken):

The boy's name is Jakque. *Ok*

The boy's name is Jakque.

("Folo copy" in the margin provides the same instruction.)

Italicize:

The girl said, "<u>Nein</u>, <u>nein</u>."

Set in bold face:

The reporter is a Phi Beta Kappa.

(If possible, hand-print corrections; otherwise clarify ambiguous handwritten letters.)

Underlines

Underline: $\underline{a}, \underline{u}, \underline{w}$

Overline: $\overline{o}, \overline{u}, \overline{m}$

The editor's finished work will look like this:

```
wyeth
hiway
1
```

The link between Interstate 17 and U.S. 39 in Swampsville will be widened to 4 lanes by the State Division of highways. The highway program for the year allocates $70,000 for acquisition of right-of-way for the multi-million dollar project, which will alter highway 163 as it enters Swampsville.

Homer C. Keller, highway department engineer for the Central District, said he was not aware that the Swampsville Improvement association had only wanted a 2-lane highway into the city. The Association contends that a four-lane highway is not needed.

The widening should cost about $14 million, keller said. The distance for 17.4 miles.

The stretch of new road will go through 3 counties. Keller reported that probably these shares of the cost will be spent in the three counties:

Adams, $3,142,389, one-sixth;

Vermillion, $2,457,679, one-eighth; and

Van Buren, $8,400,032, the rest.

The copyeditor's goals

A practiced copyeditor can flash over copy, flicking his pencil to indicate paragraphs, to cross out occasional waste phrases, and to correct misspelled words. Few mistakes will get by him.

But this kind of editing, after a time, tends to be dull and even sterile. The mediocre editor works mechanically, catching minor errors while failing to detect the big ones, like inconsistencies and omissions of fact.

The excellent editor does not disregard the little flaws. He knows that even a well-written story may have slight imperfections that distract the reader. He not only marks the misspelled word and the redundancy but sniffs the whole story for completeness and accuracy. He questions its news value. Is it worth eight paragraphs as written? Should the story be thrown away as inconsequential? Should it be rewritten for more impact on the reader?

The copyeditor who recognizes that even the best reporter may blunder recognizes that the same thing can happen to him: He may doze off and let an obvious mistake go into print. The editor must not only be skeptical of the reporter's accuracy but skeptical of his own ability to do everything right in what often has to be a hasty reading of a story.

Editing is an intellectual pursuit that requires meticulousness, careful analysis of content, judgment of story value in relation to other news, and a weighing of the significance of all news that gets into the paper. Many newsmen find it satisfying to use their brains and knowledge daily to make the news more understandable for thousands of readers.

2 Copyediting techniques

Copyeditors do uncommon work with common tools: pencils, scissors, and paste pots. Normally the newspaper provides a good stock of round, soft-lead pencils for editing. Ballpoint pens have the advantage of not smearing, but changing their marks on copypaper is impossible. So the realistic copyeditor keeps an art gum eraser at hand to correct his errant pencil marks.

Scissors and paste pots are necessary for *inserts*, pieces of copy to be added to the original story. The editor clips the story in two at the proper spot and pastes the insert to the halves of the original copy. Even without inserts a story may be considerably reorganized by cutting and pasting. Some shops also have the copyeditor paste the pages of each lengthy story together, top to bottom, to make a long, folded roll.

As for editing itself, slot men agree at most points on what they consider good copyediting. They want stories to be "fixed up" but, unless the writing is bad, they don't want them butchered and rehashed. The copyeditor has to learn the technique of the proper amount of editing. He keeps his eye on all the minutiae at the same time he watches to see that the whole story fits and flows together to give an accurate general impression. He combines good English and good sense with the paper's rules and traditions.

The leads of stories deserve particular attention, for a lead can make or break the reader's interest. If the lead doesn't click, the editor certainly should revise it.

A good copyeditor, unless squeezed by a deadline, reads each story at least twice. Often he spots errors each time through, and he should take great care to recheck any of his own rephrasing. The new sentences that he inserts should be read two or three times to make sure that the corrections themselves are not in error.

The editor ought to ask himself finally, "Does this story make sense? Are there any inadequacies? Will the reader have any important questions? Does the story read smoothly? Are all the statements properly attributed? Is there any factual error?"

He should also check to see whether the story rambles on for ten or eleven paragraphs of detail without getting essential information close to the top. This shortcoming often mars stories of strikes. The beginning usually reports who says what and how long the strike has been going on, but what the strike is all about may be buried or ignored.

The copyeditor should make changes that are necessary and quit. This means he keeps his pencil off clear and accurate writing. *Winner & Sinners* has warned editors not to change language for the sake of change. One issue noted:

> Itchy pencil . . . refers to occasional copy desk tinkering with copy for no apparent reason—a practice that sometimes makes the writing inferior, sometimes makes it outright wrong and always baffles the writer. If a hold-up man takes a picture of his colleagues with a Polaroid Land camera and the reporter writes that in that way "he was able to avoid taking the incriminating film to the corner drugstore for developing" what is gained by changing the final quoted phrase to "elsewhere"? There is actually a slight loss in sense.
>
> If a reporter writes about a chimpanzee at the Museum of Natural History that "whizzed across its acres on a red tricycle" why should "acres" be changed to "halls," which loses the idea of vastness? If a correspondent writes that a "betting man could get a dime to a nickel from almost anyone in the Western delegations" about the break-up of the Geneva conference, is there any improvement in making it "could get a wager"?
>
> Although the damage wrought in these instances may seem minor, the reader has been deprived of colorful detail; moreover, the cumulative effect on reporters of such tinkering is discouraging. Changes have to be made in copy, to be sure, but be certain that when you make a change it is definitely a change for the better and not just the work of itchy pencil.

The job of the editor, then, is to go over the copy to correct grammar, to cross out waste words and sentences, and to make the language more graceful. He should throttle clichés. Ambiguous phrasing should be hunted down and corrected.

The probing editor

The editor needs a quizzical, skeptical approach if he is to catch errors. He must keep asking as he reads, "Can this be right?" With this in mind, for example, he will question whether, as the story says, Richard Nixon was born in Massachusetts and the University of Michigan is in Kalamazoo.

Editors must check to see if needed information is omitted. A *New York Times* reporter once sent a note to the desk mentioning an editorial oversight: A story on a supersonic airliner gave only oblique reference—in the eleventh paragraph—to the name of the government agency which received the airliner designs. Knowing this kind of error should be caught by the desk, he wrote (in *Winners & Sinners*), "Every reporter is going to have an occasional lapse in fullest lucidity, and he would like to feel that he is securely backstopped. That, after all, is the copydesk's primary function."

If there is any doubt about the accuracy of his changes in a story, the editor should check with the nearest authority—the writer of the story. He might ask the reporter, "Does this improve the meaning of the story? Have I made it clearer, or have I muddled the facts?" A reporter will be furious, and has a right to be, if his copy is revised into error. It makes him look like a fool with his news sources, and it embitters the staff when an accurate story is distorted by an editor who had no first-hand knowledge of the event.

Where a reporter has used an inappropriate word, the editor should find the right one. He needs to be familiar with semantics to be sure that the words convey the intended meaning. For example, where the reporter has written "statesman," the word "politician" might be better.

There must be a steady watchfulness for libel. Every story that defames anyone—and many stories must defame should be checked to see if the defamatory phrases can be used safely under law. Chapter 12 discusses in detail the legal pitfalls that always lurk near a copyeditor.

Hoaxes are another thing to contend with. A naive reporter may write a story that sounds like a dandy. The more experienced copyeditor, however, may recall that the same story ran a decade ago and was exposed as a fake. This story needs the oblivion treatment.

Unless editors are careful a single story may get in the paper twice, causing merriment among readers. It is doubly amusing if the same stories get into the paper the same day. Occasionally, different reporters will write essentially the same story a few days apart. The writer of the second story should have read his own newspaper more carefully. But his oversight is no excuse for the copy desk to repeat the error. An alert desk must likewise kill outdated stories which did not make the paper. A story announcing last night's event as "tonight" is bad news for the participants, the frustrated audience, and the newspaper.

Editors also have to watch for advertising that masquerades as news. Since newspapers sell advertising, news stories should mention advertisers only when they make news. For example, if a meeting is going to take place at a hotel, the reporter has to say which hotel. This "advertising" is unavoidable and therefore permissible. Glowing descriptions of the hotel, however, should be crossed out of news copy.

It is even harder but more important to eliminate propaganda. All kinds of people try to sneak their points of view into the paper under the guise of news, and this is most apparent during election time when dozens of events are staged to attract attention. The editor

should sift through all the fakery and try to stick to the issues in the reports he prints.

Sometimes an inexperienced reporter will quote a news source too much and let the source misuse the news columns to further himself or his cause. The editor gives this material its proper weight, which is sometimes nothing.

Eight pointers

Double-check names.   If the copyeditor has any doubt about the spelling of a name, he should look it up, and he should be sure that a name is spelled consistently through the story. A person should not be Whelan in the first paragraph and Whalen in the second. The editor should watch for a common lapse associated with unusual names: The reporter uses a person's full name in the lead but mistakenly substitutes the first name for the last in the rest of the story. For example, the lead may refer to the president of Harvard University as Dr. Nathan M. Pusey. From then on, however, he is Dr. Nathan instead of Dr. Pusey. The copyeditor should catch this blunder.

Attribute facts properly. Almost anything that cannot be witnessed by the reporter should be attributed to some person. The "almost" is essential to remember because often stories contain facts neither observed by reporters nor found through records, and so there is no attribution. Attribution is unnecessary when the source obviously is telling the truth. For example, it is silly to attribute to a university president the employment of every single faculty member. The university is not going to announce an appointment by a news release and then back out of it, so phrases like "the president announced" are unnecessary.

Produce clean copy.   Stories sent to the composing room must be readable. Hurriedly scrawled editorial changes make the printer guess at the scribbles—and make wrong guesses—or force him to throw the story back to the desk. Either way the paper can lose accuracy or time. If the deskman must make complicated handwritten changes, he should type out the most involved ones and paste the retyped material over the messy original.

"Duck it."   Sometimes an editor spots a minor misstatement in a story, and the reporter who wrote the story is not around for verification. Any other check might take fifteen minutes. The item is not worth that much time so the editor "ducks it" by omitting the statement. A story may say, "Jones, who moved here in 1953, has served on the county board for 17 years." The copyeditor may trust "17 years" but doubt "1953." How could Jones have won an election so soon? So the editor ducks the problem by changing the sentence to "Jones has served on the county board for 17 years."

Simplify language.   Newspapers are not written for morons, but for people who want to get the news and comment in easy-to-read form. Simpler words should replace involved ones like "inextricable," "dichotomy," and "tangential." Language even for an intellectual audience should be precise and readable, not pretentious.

Reporters sometimes get caught up in the special language of the fields they cover. Court reporters, for instance, may write "filed a demurrer," "stayed the execution," or "granted a continuance." Such terms may be hard for a layman to grasp, and the editor who thinks the story should interest the ordinary reader will either change the wording himself or send it back to the reporter for translation.

Recognize your own prejudices. Copyeditors need to double-check themselves to be sure they do not make decisions to chop one story and inflate another because of personal prejudice. Some editors who control newspaper content favor stories that concern their personal hobbies. A man who loves to sail may run an unusual number of stories about boats and the sea. Such prejudices are basically harmless, although they could make the paper look amateurish. Sometimes, however, an editor may intensely dislike a senator or fear that the nation is moving rapidly toward socialism. He may edit the news to make the senator look foolish or to emphasize his own political views. This kind of editing is harmful and unprofessional.

Don't trust your memory completely. A copyeditor is often tempted to pencil into a story a fact that he thinks will improve the article. He should insert these facts, however, only when absolutely sure of them. If he isn't certain, he should look up the information in the clipping file or a reference book.

Be sure copy is fair and tasteful. Balancing objective reporting and interpretation is a continual problem, but even if a story is primarily interpretive it should be fair. Snide, belittling comments should be removed.

Rebuttal from criticized persons should be included or run as a separate story nearby. Copy should also remain in good taste. Taste is difficult to assess, but most editors have a rule-of-thumb: A paper read by all kinds of people, including children, should soften or eliminate the most brutal or intimate details.

While this advice is generally good, it doesn't always work. As an illustration, some papers handle a sex offense by referring to a "morals charge." But such an all-encompassing term actually may be unfair to the accused, because the phrase covers a wide spectrum of sins. In such cases some editors try to be a little more specific without being salacious. Others simply do not print "morals" arrests except in cases when they can't avoid it, as when omitting such news about a public figure might bring a charge of covering-up for him.

The copyeditor must always be thinking of how to make the news readable for his readers. He points up the local angle whenever possible. He revives listless writing and chops out ponderous language to make the sentences brisk and the story a pleasure to follow. On the other hand, he may have to add a phrase to make the story clearer or to tone down lurid writing. A good slogan is "make copy brisk but not brusque, vivid but not lurid."

**Color
and completeness**

The reader in Oshkosh may sit up when he finds a story with an Oshkosh angle in it. Localization can be overdone, of course, like this:

```
The brother-in-law of a man who lived in Oshkosh in 1929 was
arrested today in Dallas on a charge of panhandling.
```

But if an Oshkosh native wins a Nobel Prize, the Oshkosh paper better have his place of birth in the lead, not in the ninth paragraph as it probably came over the wire.

Localizing often requires some juggling of paragraphs. Sometimes it requires only a phrase inserted high in the story:

```
        (including Peoria)
Fifteen cities have been awarded million-dollar grants to
help relieve poverty.
```

In other cases it will require restructuring the story considerably, perhaps rewriting the lead or inserting paragraph seven after paragraph one. Feature writers have a habit of writing long introductions before getting to the heart of the story. An editor often can chop out whole paragraphs at the beginning of such pieces, just as he can trim the tail end of many news stories.

Whenever possible the stories should be organized to pinpoint the significance for the reader. Most of us read stories, as Wilbur Schramm has pointed out, because we want to be rewarded: We want to know what will affect our pocketbooks, to know what has happened to our friends and acquaintances, to know what might please us or upset us. The reporter writes his stories with these ideas in mind, and the copyeditor fixes the reporter's oversights:

```
        (property)
School taxes will go up $1.5 million next year, the board
of education decided last night. The new rate means that
if a resident paid $200 in school taxes this year,
he will pay $224 next year.
```

Because the editor knows that every reader has certain areas of ignorance, he often explains what the reporter thought obvious. "Died of nephritis" needs an explanatory phrase. If the story mentions District IV schools, tell the reader, at least roughly, what District IV covers. If the story mentions Albert Einstein, add an identifying phrase. The story must remind as well as inform readers, and the brightest of them have gaps in their knowledge.

The reporter, as has been said many times, is the eyes, ears, hands, nose and tongue of the reader. If the reporter does not describe the look, the sound, the feel, the smell, or the taste of something that needs these descriptions, the editor should get him to include it.

But the copyeditor occasionally thinks that a reporter, striving for vividness, has given an incorrect tone. Perhaps the reporter unconsciously chose words the editor thinks will sound snide to the reader. The editors of the *Cleveland Press* once noted that reporters often used the word "peacenik." The editors believed that the word "has a built-in sneer," and pointed out that "there is nothing wrong with being for peace."

Even the context of words may alter the tone of a story. For example, a report of a speech may be filled with attributive phrases like "he roared," "Jackson thundered," and "he shouted." It is possible that the speaker did roar, thunder, and shout. But in print these words make the man sound wild, and he may not have been wild at all. He may simply have had a strong voice or been trying to reach the listeners sitting far behind the reporter's front row seat.

On the other hand, a reporter may turn in a biographical story filled with syrupy phrases that make a rather ordinary person appear to be a saint. The deletion of a half dozen adjectives in these cases usually makes the tone ring true. No one should assume, however, that the tone of stories need always be coldly factual. A funny incident should be reported in a funny way. A story on a political session may be irreverent. And a story on a funeral generally should be dignified and restrained.

The *New York Times* started a story on a St. Patrick's Day parade with: "Irishmen, regardless of race, creed or color, marched down Fifth Avenue today."

In a story on the keynote speech at the Democratic National convention in 1952, Red Smith wrote: "The Democratic party was smitten tonight with the jawbone of an ass."

A somber funeral story might include: "The senator's wife sat dry-eyed through the services, occasionally biting her lip to keep back the tears."

Of course every story should have the essential facts as well as the right tone. The reader is interested in the overall view of an event, but he also expects the story to answer his reasonable questions. If the reporter doesn't have the answer, the story should say so: "Petersen's age was not learned."

Balancing the reporter's judgment

Polishing pointers

Sometimes the editor's pencil and willingness to restructure are not enough to revive a story. The sentences are long-winded, the quotes are ponderous, and the story seems to drone on. The copyeditor has to read each paragraph twice to get the foggiest understanding of what the writer was driving at. The story demands rewriting, and it should go back to the reporter or another staffer with specific instructions on how to improve it.

Quotations that look brief in copy take up an alarming amount of space when squeezed into a column width. The copyeditor can boil down long-winded quotations by combining material, omitting by ellipsis, or using partial quotes:

"The dam, which is designed to bring vast blessings to the people of Central Illinois and which will avoid terrifying floods, will cost $8 million and be built within two years," the governor said.

The quote could be paraphrased:

The dam will cost $8 million and take two years to build, the governor said.

Another possibility would be:

"The dam . . . will cost $8 million and be built within two years," the governor said.

Quotation marks do suggest authenticity, but too many of them make the report look patched together. Quotes are the seasoning of the story, not the meat.

Reporters that keep interrupting their own stories put the reader in a coma with the comma. An involved sentence that stitches facts together with commas needs editing:

The Tobiason boy, 8 years old and fourth grader at the new Leal school, said that his mother, the former Ann Davis who was Miss America 14 years ago, had planned to pick him up at 4 p.m. at the school.

The reference to her former title can be inserted elsewhere.

Other reporters string identifications of people throughout a story. This is noted particularly on the sports page. In the first paragraph the football player is simply "a halfback," in the second he is "the native of Florida," in the third "the 205-pounder," in the fourth "the Big Ten's leading ground-gainer," and in the fifth "the junior economics major." Such detailed identification, if used at all, should form a two or three sentence paragraph of background information.

Redundancies are harder to spot than quotes or identification tags, and they are more worrisome. They waste space and bring snickers from readers. Obvious ones like "killed to death" rarely creep into copy, but subtler ones like "widow of the late John Smith" are unsettlingly common. "Autopsy of the body" suggests that autopsies are performed on things other than bodies. "Graves of dead soldiers will be decorated" indicates that some soldiers are buried alive.

The correct use of words can raise interesting problems. A dictionary, of course, is a good guide, but sometimes a "correctly" used word will convey the wrong sense. An editorial writer once referred to a major religious denomination as a "sect." If connotation is ignored, this is a "correct" use of the word. But many readers were incensed, for they viewed the word "sect" as a term for little flocks that convene in abandoned stores.

Subject-verb disagreement.   It is not unusual to see a story with "the council *meet* today at noon" or "the group *is* going to take separate cars to their hotels."

Six more flaws to fix

Pronouns. Whenever the copyeditor runs across *he, she, it,* or *they* he should check to see if the right person or thing is identified. If there is doubt, a suitable noun, not a pronoun, should be used.

Illogical dependent clauses.   Watch sentences like "A graduate of Harvard, he is the father of eight children." Being a father has nothing to do with attendance at Harvard.

Double meanings.   There is always someone around who will spot the secondary—and possibly racy—meaning of a phrase. These double meanings amuse readers, but they detract from professionalism. Even a relatively harmless double meaning embarrasses the parties involved, including the editor. During a presidential campaign, a headline accidentally suggested a domestic problem for Richard M. Nixon's wife, whose nickname is Pat.

Can't Stand Pat,
Nixon Declares

Editorializing.   Any trace of personal opinion or a value judgment should be eliminated, unless the story is a feature or news analysis.

Unlikely quotes.   Sometimes reporters invent quotes and the unfortunate result is a sentence or two with a hollow ring. A baseball team manager noted for his linguistic errors, for example, may be quoted as saying, "We were in a desperate position in the third inning, but Bocko Jennings, our superlative third baseman, made what must be the best play of the year, allowing us to escape without damage." This unbelievable quote should be scratched and the facts put in as straight news: The manager said Bocko Jennings' spectacular play saved the game.

Occasionally, a reporter writes that more than one person said the same thing: "John Adams and Peter Farrel said, 'I think the foreign policy of the nation is clearly a menace.'" One of them might say it, but not both.

Series.   Check a series of several items in one sentence for a surplus verb. "He is a determined golf player, a collector of antique clocks and often reads a detective story at night." To clear up the awkwardness, the copyeditor could change it to: "He is a determined golf player and a collector of antique clocks. He often reads a detective story at night."

Rechecking details

The copyeditor obviously checks spelling and punctuation with particular attention to the placement of quotation marks and apostrophes. *Its* and *it's* always need a second look to see if they have been used correctly. Every possessive must have the apostrophe in the right place. The editor even does a little arithmetic to check totals given in a story. For example, if the reporter's copy states that two objects weigh three pounds and that each weighs eighteen ounces the editor should start asking questions. An editor must not hesitate to ask the reporter to double-check something that looks as though it might be wrong. If the story is from a wire service, a query to the wire service should resolve the doubt.

Saving space

When copyeditors rewrite extensively, they are tempted to pencil whole new paragraphs between the lines of copy. This short cut usually turns out to be the hard way for the typesetter and proofreader. If the copy needs extensive revision, it should be returned to the originating editor for a rewrite. The copyeditor, however, may try to rewrite a few sentences in the story and discover that one new sentence includes the gist of three or four.

Any copyeditor must spend a good share of his time reducing copy—not because he would not like to run more detail but because there simply is no room for it. Editing to save space means applying the scalpel, not the meat ax. Some copy butchers would merely whack off six inches from the story's end and send the remains to the printer. The skillful editor, however, recreates. For example, he takes off the last two paragraphs, removes the fourth, combines two rather long sentences into one of moderate length, takes a phrase from two or three different sentences, and makes a long quotation into a short one. The marked copy below shows how the editor in such condensation leaves as much fact as possible, sacrificing only the least significant details.

The cutting may not seem like much, but it removed about six lines of copy. This means that the story is about an inch and a half shorter in type and may now just fill the allotted space. Furthermore, a dozen stories each shortened that much would make room for another eighteen-inch story.

WASHINGTON-(AP)-The bodies of two crewmen of the U. S. Navy

reconnaissance plane shot down by North Korea have been found in the

Sea of Japan, informed sources in Japan said Thursday.

A search ~~over thousands of square miles~~ for the plane and its
31 crewmen has been under way since (it) ~~the four~~ engine, ~~propeller-driven~~
~~EC-121~~ was reported missing Monday after North Korea said it had downed
the aircraft for allegedly violating its territory.

The massive search, which earlier had turned up only ~~shrapnel~~
~~shredded~~ bits of the plane, discovered ~~fuselage and other material, had found~~ no sign of the
29 other crewmen. Officials doubted that any ~~of the men~~ survived.

The sources said they had no information on where the bodies
were found. The debris picked up Wednesday was found about 120 miles
southeast of the north Korean coast.

The bodies of the two men were clothed in flying suits but not ~~were~~
~~not wearing~~ life jackets, Japan's Kyodo News Service reported. Kyodo
~~which did not give its source,~~ also said the bodies were picked up by
the U. S. destroyer Tucker.

~~The recovery of the bodies came as the world waited for~~ Presi-
dent Nixon has made no statement about the incident ~~to break the calculated public silence he instituted after~~
~~North Korea declared it had destroyed the plane.~~

~~Officials indicated Wednesday~~ the President was expected to
issue some sort of protest to North Korea, ~~and there has been no evidence of a change.~~ But no decision has been reported about how this
would be done.

Every newspaper should have a *style book*. This term does not
refer here to a book on writing style but rather to a booklet put out
by a newspaper telling how capitalization, abbreviation, and punctuation are handled in news stories for that paper. Reporters are
supposed to follow this set of rules, or *style*, but sometimes they
don't. The editor must then correct their errors, so he needs to be
thoroughly familiar with the style book but willing to look up an
obscure point whenever there is any doubt—or argument.

Guidebooks for accuracy

The consistency established by the style book prevents the meticulous reader from being annoyed when a story spells a proper name two or three different ways in as many paragraphs—or abbreviates a word one time and spells it out the next.

If a newspaper does not have its own style book the editors may use a book published by another paper, such as the thorough one published by the *New York Times*. The Associated Press and United Press International have joined forces to publish a widely used style book. Since all copy from AP and UPI coming into newsrooms conforms to this style, it would be wasteful for a paper that used mostly wire copy to make many changes in it.

Accuracy of copy requires several other reference books. Two of them, a medium-sized dictionary and the *World Almanac*, should be at arm's length. The need of the dictionary is obvious. The *Almanac* is the poor man's encyclopedia. It gives an editor quick access to thousands of facts on recent history, dates, biographies, and records. Today a one-volume paperback edition of an encyclopedia is even available to save the editor from getting up to consult the multivolume, recent set that should be nearby.

A good, unabridged dictionary and the city directories should be close by. Most newspapers have such books in the middle of the newsroom where everyone can get to them quickly. In addition, some editors use a thesaurus to help find the right synonym for an awkward word in a headline or story.

The following essential but less frequently used books should be easily accessible in the newspaper's library or reference room (sometimes still called "the morgue").

Congressional Directory
Area telephone books
Various kinds of *Who's Who*, such as *Who's Who in the East*
United States Postal Guide
Blue Book or *Red Book* for every state the newspaper serves—to
    provide information about state government
Dictionary of American Biography
Current Biography
A grammar, such as E. L. Callihan's *Grammar for Journalists*
Facts on File
A complete, modern atlas, such as the *National Geographic Atlas of
    the World*
American Labor Yearbook
A geographical dictionary, such as the *Macmillan World Gazetteer
    and Geographical Dictionary*
New York Times Index, and back issues of *Times* on microfilm
Statistical Abstract of the U. S.
International Motion Picture Almanac
King James and modern editions of the Bible
Poor's Public Utilities
Moody's Railroads
Encyclopaedia of the Social Sciences

Various sports record books and military directories

A book on good usage, such as *Current American Usage*, by Margaret M. Bryant; *A Dictionary of American-English Usage*, by Margaret Nicholson (based on a famous English work by H. W. Fowler); *A Dictionary of Contemporary American Usage*, by Bergen and Cornelia Evans; or *Modern American Usage*, by Wilson Follett

The largest newspapers have even more reference books, and Dr. Eleanor Blum's *Reference Books in the Mass Media*, a paperback, lists all of them. Some are used so rarely that many newspapers don't need to own them. However, a telephone call or a quick trip by a copy boy to a public library can put an editor in touch with almost any reference book.

3 Writing headlines

Headlines have been compared to road signs, advertising slogans, and store windows. All these have in common the task of seizing attention and putting a message across swiftly. That is what a good newspaper head does. The first and most important purpose of a headline is to inform the reader quickly. The well-written head tells him immediately the gist of the accompanying story.

When it is said that we are a nation of headline skimmers, the tone is usually derogatory. The other side of that criticism, however, is that skimming heads is what makes possible our rapid comprehension of the news, since literally no one can read all the stories that are processed each day. If the heads do their most important job—rapid summary—the careful skimmer will get the general drift of events; and yet he can slow up for a story he judges worth more careful reading.

A second important goal of headlines is also related to their billboard function. Headlines must sell. On newstands in competitive cities front page headlines tend to sell one paper instead of another. In monopoly cities they may push a reader to buy a paper instead of skipping it. But on the inside pages of every newspaper, headlines "sell" the reader to start reading a story. Philosophically, the primary function of the free press in a democracy is not to make money but to inform citizens. But in our society the paper must be profitable to remain alive—and lively, so the head that sells is significant.

Related to both informing and selling is a third function: grading, or evaluating, the news. One head shouts that this story is important. Another suggests quietly that this one might be of some interest as well. Even the size and style of type help communicate to the reader the importance and quality of the news—whether it is a cataclysmic disaster or a pleasant afternoon tea. A fuller explanation of how the editor evaluates news appears in chapter 6.

To stimulate the reader's artistic sense is a final purpose of headlines. Dull heads make a dull page. But graphic artistry is much more complex than merely replacing dullness with brightness.

Headlines may add to the clutter of ugly or confusing pages. But when heads are well-written and well-placed in styles that have been thoughtfully designed, the pages are clean and good-looking. Indeed, the whole personality of a paper is set by the consistent use of heads day after day, and a sudden, drastic change in heads may make a subscriber feel he has lost a familiar friend.

Hazards in heads

One of the newspaper's most vulnerable points is the headline. Readers may grumble about the way a paper covers the news but often their complaint boils down to dislike of the heads used.

Simple inattention can make heads which read two ways, sometimes ludicrously. Here are two published examples which seem to speak of mailmen who are stolen and belts which are hurt:

**Stolen Postman's Truck
Recovered in N. Jersey**

**Couple Hurt
Seat Belts Aid
In Collision**

More than one reporter has complained that his story was all right—and it was the head on it that distorted. For example, in *Editor & Publisher* James Steed of White Plains, New York, complained: "For too long the reporter has had to explain to the public and his readership that 'someone back on the copy desk' makes up the headlines and if they don't match up with the story there is nothing the reporter can do about it." Steed pointed out that since newspapers print corrections on stories, they should likewise run "a correction when the headline conveys the wrong meaning." He urged that the anonymity and immunity be removed from the headwriter who "messes up a good story by putting the wrong tag on it."

Popular confidence in a newspaper can be seriously shaken by an attack on headlines. For example, at a gathering of the New York State Council of Churches, Governor Nelson Rockefeller criticized a headline on the front page of the *New York Times* for misrepresenting his statement about a state lottery. Rockefeller, who had long opposed such a lottery, said he had explained to a reporter that if the people approved a lottery in a referendum and the legislature then passed a bill, he would study and possibly sign it. The *Times* editor used a short, punchy verb in the head over the resulting story:

**Rockefeller Bows
On State Lottery**

The secondary head, or deck, on the resulting story did qualify the main head with some of the governor's words:

**Would Go Along Reluctantly
With 'Reasonable' Bill**

But Rockefeller contended that the main head oversimplified his position and would be all that most readers would catch. Such attacks by public figures erode the public's confidence in newspapers. Admittedly, some headwriters do distort or bias the news, or they editorialize. But there are built-in dangers in headwriting even for the careful copyeditor of goodwill. He has to struggle with the limitations of both space and brief words to convey a fair and accurate impression.

Perhaps oversimplification is the greatest threat in headlines. When the news is complex, the reporter often oversimplifies in writing a tight lead. The copyeditor's job is to polish and tighten that more, if possible. Then he has to condense it still further into a half dozen words or fewer for the headline. The subtleties inevitably get squeezed out, which was at the base of Governor Rockefeller's complaint. All that the honest desk man can do is avoid distortion as best he can, changing the angle if necessary in order to keep from oversimplifying.

A second danger in headlines is emphasis on a minor angle of a story. A common complaint of speakers is that a reporter takes some minor point, even an aside, and builds a big story around it. The fault is compounded if the head plays up this angle, perhaps in oversimplified form. What the speaker and audience both understood as almost a joke may, for example, be blazoned:

Blasts Commie Profs

Readers who were there—and perhaps the speaker's future audiences—will then be re-convinced that newspapers distort and sensationalize.

Distrust of headlines led Mrs. John F. Kennedy, widow of the President, to ask *Look* editors to serialize a book about his last days in not more than two or three installments. Her argument was that critical comments about some prominent persons, including President Johnson, would be fairest in the context of long installments. She feared that if the story came out in small pieces, newspapers would repeatedly pick up minor angles and give them sensational headlines.

Another danger in headlines is overplay. Too much emphasis on a story usually results from a bad choice of type, but vivid headline words may also overdramatize. Another factor is news flow. A story which would deserve a small one-column head inside on an ordinary day may be overplayed under several columns on the front page when news is dull. According to a tradition, which is probably passing, some newspapers run a full-width banner head across the front page every day. (The *banner* is also called a *streamer* or *line*.) This tradition inevitably overplays some stories. A reader might suspect that some of the banners in figure 4-1 distort the news.

Underplay, of course, is also a threat. Admitting that there is no universal standard of correct play, fair-minded editors nevertheless acknowledge that some papers do not give certain stories the space or heads they deserve. This may be the result of policy or simply of ignorance—maybe the desk man does not realize that the coup in such-and-such a country really affects his readers. Some editors knowingly order small heads on racial riots in other communities, on the theory that large heads would "stir things up" at home.

Fig. 3-1. Banners. Though street sales are of declining importance, a number of newspapers still use banner headlines like these, clear across the front page, sometimes with other banners or streamers above or below.

Heads of quality

Notwithstanding criticisms, most newspaper headwriters do a good job, day in, day out. They may often compose routine or dull heads, but they are accurate. Nothing better illustrates such good, ordinary headlines—unimaginative, perhaps, but fair—than the latest edition of any large daily.

Kudos for headwriting usually go to the writers who have a flair for saying the difficult with style. The head which draws the envy of other professionals usually displays unique imagery or wit. The neophyte who wants to distinguish himself as headwriter should try to develop a colorful way of putting things in a few words; he will sometimes write corn, but he may develop a valuable talent. The headwriter should probe nearly every story for something amusing or clever that can be brought up to a headline. In some instances, as for an obituary, it would be in bad taste. But some real effort to be droll or even funny will produce an occasional gem. Here, for example, are several heads which play on words cleverly:

**The Mao Clinic: China
Sends MDs to Paddies
To Cure Political Ills**

The Reign in Spain Is Plainly on the Wane

**Lake Carriers Clear Decks
For Battle with Railroads**

Tigers Get 9 Goose Eggs for Easter

**Airport in New Zealand
Definitely Isn't for Birds**

**Heat Turned on Cook
In Very Short Order**

Modern head styles

Even before the words of a head are chosen, several other decisions face the copydesk. Normally the slot man or news editor makes these choices almost automatically. Chapter 9 takes up typographic points in detail, but here are some brief guidelines on modern practice.

Type face and size

Modern newspapers use head types which are clean and easily readable, as is apparent in figure 4-3. *Sans serif* types (without decorative lines, dots, and squiggles) are popular; so-called *modern* or *transitional* types—especially Bodoni—also are often employed because their sharp, bold lines are quickly grasped. Condensed type (squeezed so that many letters will fit into a column) was popular a few decades ago, but the trend is to larger sizes. This movement toward display types which are big, legible, and attractive complicates the problem for the writer who has much to say in little space.

Number of lines

The spread of horizontal make-up, which uses multi-column heads almost exclusively, brings wide use of the single line three or more columns wide. But two-line heads are by far the most frequent. Though three lines in major headlines are still common, probably less so than a generation ago, four lines are rare.

Width

Heads are growing wider as "magazine style" becomes more popular. The traditional "Civil War head" of numerous parts was one column wide and, it seemed, almost a column long (fig. 4-2). Today only a few papers still hold to a tradition of frequent one-column heads. Headlines of two, three, and four columns are widely employed on most American newspapers. Use of two and even three heads of six and eight columns on a single page is common.

Style

Aside from the number and length of lines, several other elements set the style of an individual headline.
One factor is arrangement of lines. Should they be even on the left or should they step in on one side? Or should they be stepped in on

both sides? The answer will determine how modern or streamlined a head looks. The *stepped* head, in which succeeding lines of about the same length are stepped over to the right, is still used. But the *flush left* head—all lines evened up at the left—has been most popular for decades now, because it can be written more speedily.

If the first line is full and another line or two are stepped in to make a trapezoid shape, the head is called an inverted pyramid. This style is usually used as a subordinate part of a heading, but it sometimes stands alone as the main head.

Lines of varying length are not always set flush left, with ragged right edge; instead, centering each line can make an effective head. This style is not much used in this country but is common abroad, as in the London *Daily Telegraph*.

Stepped Head **Takes Lines of** **Equal Length**	**Centered Head** **Finds Little** **Editorial Support**
Flush Left **Lines Can** **Vary a Bit**	**Inverted Pyramid Style** **Rarely Used In** **Main Head**

Another question of style concerns capitalization. The two older forms are "all caps"—with every letter a capital—or "caps and lowers," the conventional capitalization of book titles. But the *lower case* head, which appears to be growing in popularity because of speed of setting and reading, uses only one capital letter—for the first word. Except for proper nouns, other words are entirely lower case—that is, small letters—for quick reading.

ALL CAPS SEEM **TOO BOLD** **TODAY**	**Caps and Lowers** **May Soon Be** **On Uppers**	**Lower case rises** **to prominence** **in U. S.**

The other most obvious variable in determining the shape or appearance of the head is the number of parts. Accompanying the main head may be one or more smaller headings to lead the eye down into the story. These parts of a headline are called *decks* (or sometimes *banks* or *drops*). The strong trend has been towards the single deck, especially in one-column heads. While some papers use three or four decks in a head, two is the maximum on most papers. Typically the story is told in the first part, or *top*, and further detail follows in the second part, which is sometimes called simply *the deck*. (See fig. 4-4.)

As decks have declined in popularity, the *kicker* has become popular. It is a head of from one to several words, frequently with an underlining rule centered above the main head or to the left of it. Writing of decks and kickers will be considered later in this chapter.

In summary, a head in small type, narrow measure, with several decks of stepped lines looks old-fashioned. The modern head tends

Chicago

VOL. XVIII.   CHICAGO, SATURDAY, APRIL 15, 18

Fig. 3-2. Civil War head. It was hard to skim headlines a century ago. To continue past the head into the story took stamina, though no doubt every reader in 1865 continued past the head of this item in the **Chicago Tribune** of April 15.

Fig. 3-3. Typical headlines. Ordinary heads from wide variety of papers illustrate the similarity of styles across the country. Note that all are flush left.

Wider Probes Due on UFOs

Astronauts Rehearse Maneuvers

Employe of Hospital Is Held as Suspect In 21 Arson Cases

GOP Watches Activities Of Rival Party

Only Republican Interest Centers on Comptroller

POSTSCRIPT.

4 O'CLOCK A. M.

TERRIBLE NEWS

President Lincoln Assassinated at Ford's Theater.

A REBEL DESPERADO SHOOTS HIM THROUGH THE HEAD AND ESCAPES.

Secretary Seward and Major Fred Seward Stabbed by Another Desperado.

THEIR WOUNDS ARE PRONOUNCED NOT FATAL.

Full Details of the Terrible Affair.

UNDOUBTED PLAN TO MURDER SECRETARY STANTON.

Very Latest—The President is Dying.

[Special Dispatch to the Chicago Tribune.]
WASHINGTON, April 14, 1865.
The President and Mrs. Lincoln were at Ford's Theater listening to the performance of the "American Cousin," occupying a box in the second tier. At the close of the third act, a person

GOP Watches Activities Of Rival Party

Only Republican Interest
Centers on Comptroller

Some Fathers Find Loafing Worthwhile

Jobs Pay Less Than Welfare

A Rough U. N. Session Expected
U. S. Diplomats Bracing for Stormy Debate on Viet Nam

Fig. 3-4. Use of decks. Subordinate decks are used in various ways in relation to the main head or deck.

to be in a large and clear face, flush left and several columns wide, in lower case, and accompanied by not more than one subordinate deck.

Head schedules

If the headwriters had to ponder all these decisions for every headline, they would never get out a daily paper. Even on magazines, where longer deadlines permit debate on head decisions, many choices are routinized. On newspapers, the editors select few head styles for regular use and put them into a list or *head schedule*. This listing of headlines facilitates the choice of head and also provides a coding which permits fast communication with the printers. (See fig. 4-5.)

The typical head schedule is a graduated listing of big heads down to little. For example, a 48-point head may be called "A," a 36-point "B," a 30-point "C," and so on. Then the copyreader has only to write the letter to instruct the printer. (A "point" is one seventy-second of an inch. Seventy-two point type, then, is one inch high. Thirty-six point is a half-inch. Other details will be explained in chapter 9.)

With each heading on the schedule—or in the copyreader's memory—must be the "head count," the number of characters or units in a line. Normally this count refers to the maximum number of letters which will fit into one column, and the copyreader writes lines with a count a little below that; if the head is two, three, or more columns, he gets the count by multiplying by two, three, etc. (How copyeditors count fat and thin letters will be discussed later in this chapter.)

Here, for example, is the top of the head schedule for the *Rochester* (N. Y.) *Times-Union*:

Name	Character Count	Type Size Indicated
No. 2	9	(36-point Bodoni)
No. 3	10-1/2	(30-point Bodoni)
No. 4	11-1/2	(24-point Bodoni)

Fig. 3-5. Head schedule. Chicago Sun-Times "hed sked," typically, gives counts for types ranging from 120-point down to 12.

120 point; count 2½ per column

STRIKE

96 point; count 3 per column

DR. KIN

72 point; count 5 per column

Water Sho

60 point; count 6½ per column

Depots Destr

42 point; count 9 per column

Hiking Mortgages

30 point; count 11 per column

Law Student Internshi

#43

Britain Defends Pound

#K34

ABSENTEE VOTE

Major Crisis Shakes Little San Marino

#28

Rebels Execute Chief Of Junta, Nigeria Hears

#19

Vatican Raps Speculation On Birth Decisions

#14

Thai Officials Tell Of Foiling Red Plot

#15 FREAK

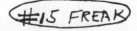

This means that the large No. 2 head permits up to 9 letters and spaces in a column. For two columns the count is obviously 18—perhaps a bit more, because the copyeditor gains the space of the rule between columns. The No. 3 head has slightly smaller type, so 10-1/2 units of this fit into a column. And so on. (On the copy, two lines after the number, like an equals sign, indicate a two-line head, and three lines a three-line head. Thus 4= is a two-line No. 4 head.)

The parenthetical indication of type size in the *Times-Union* schedule is unusual. But even if a schedule does have a reminder of type size, it is important that the copyeditor memorize the faces and sizes of the heads as he then can quickly construct offbeat headlines.

In fact, too often the whole head schedule is not in print. The authors have worked for three large dailies that had no formal printed head schedules. Copydesk men keep the schedule in their heads, and a newcomer must learn the heads and counts from them. The better practice is to have examples of the heads run off on proof paper, distributed to concerned staff members, and posted near the copydesk.

The newcomer to a copydesk naturally learns and follows the heading system in use. To revise the head schedule takes the judgment of newsmen familiar with the personality of the paper; and sometimes typographers may aid in a complete redesigning of the type dress. The general rule is to choose types which harmonize, and that usually means sticking to one family of type. The regular face is used in different sizes, and more variety is introduced by using italic, bold face, ultra-bold, and condensed versions of the basic face. Sometimes a second style of type will complement the basic one, as, for example, sans serif with a modern face. Use of three or more faces leads quickly to chaos.

Too many head sizes also will disrupt the schedule. A dozen probably will suffice for most stories. The head schedule becomes too lengthy and complicated for practical use if jammed with every head ever used. The desk then has to be prepared, and have the liberty, to create different arrangements of type for features and other special needs. Using that *Times-Union* schedule, for example, a copyeditor could write a four-column headline of two lines in 36-point Bodoni, with a 24-point kicker in Bodoni Roman or Ultra. He would simply have to give brief instructions to the printer beyond the head schedule code.

A knowledge of type enables the copyeditor to write offbeat headlines. While he must take care not to introduce confusion and ugliness, the imaginative deskman can create variety and freshness with unorthodox new heads, such as those in figure 4-6.

Basic rules for heads

Label heads

Many of the world's papers have accustomed readers to heads which are mere labels. A London paper, for example, may proclaim in 18- or 24-point type, "Parliamentary Debate" or "Death at Chamonix." Most American readers find such label heads dull, but an editor overseas can argue with some point that they do not give the whole story away. There may even be some tendency in the

The view from above
Water, water everywhere...

2 Women Try Vainly to Save 3d on IND Tracks

That Station in Wales
(Llanfairpwllewyngyllgogerye etc.)
Trips Up a Teletypist

At 9:24 A.M. yesterday,
the Reuters press agency

Brooklyn Train Hits Her as
She's Almost Pulled Up—
28 Others on Platform

Fig. 3-6. Off-beat heads. The copyeditor who knows his head types can create unorthodox headlines such as these, which are probably not on a head schedule.

United States, as newsstand competition diminishes, for the American editor to use more label heads. The well-edited *Des Moines Register*, for example, has recently used a number of verbless headlines like this:

Nuns' China Ordeal:
Tears and Death

Another *Register* example which at first seems to have a verb actually uses a gerund (verbal employed as noun):

Mobilizing of
Guard After
Negro Death

The main stream of American head-writing, however, emphasizes the punchy, dramatic, summary headline. American readers would immediately sense something wrong if they met this headline:

Punchy heads

The Congressmen Were in a Disagreement
On the Housing Legislation

It is wrong because it is past tense; it has no active verb with subject; and it has several articles. Furthermore, most of the words are too long for a conventional head.

An American feels much more at home if he sees the subject summarized this way:

Solons Split
On Race Bill

This head is in the present tense; a concrete noun is followed by a strong, active verb; and the articles have been sliced out. This same example, however, has some weaknesses of headwriting. "Solons" is *headlinese*, or jargon, which many copydesks frown on. "Split" may be read here as a verb in the past tense or an adjective, and it doubtless overstates the debate which the reporter discussed. And while "race bill" has punch, it introduces an oversimplification and perhaps even connotations which the more complex language avoids.

Abbreviating

How does the copyeditor decide what to put in the abbreviated key sentence which is the headline?

As the reporter has tried to get the gist of the story into a lead which summarizes the event, the headwriter now boils that sentence down to fit the count on the head schedule. In theory, at its simplest, he switches the sentence into the present tense and eliminates articles and time-place references. The remaining skeleton is typically subject, verb, and, perhaps, direct or indirect object.

Following the example above, let us say the wire carries this lead:

WASHINGTON—Congress today launched debate on the controversial bill providing for an expansion of racial integration in housing.

This lead might become a two-line head:

Congress Debates
Housing Bill

But since the second line is a little short, one writer might stretch it a bit by juggling grammar:

Congress Debates
Bill on Housing

Another might prefer to add information:

Congress Debates
Race Housing Bill

It can be objected that this head is rather general and imprecise, but the objection applies to the lead as well. The head properly condenses the lead.

Some slot men would contend that the first words of the head should carry the main punch of the story. "Congress" is dull. So they would ask the copyeditor to substitute a more powerful word:

Race Housing
Bill Debated

But this makes the verb passive, and other editors would argue that the verb must be active.

Rules and reality

This difference illustrates two points about headwriting: (1) "Inviolable" rules sometimes collide head-on, and a choice has to be made as to which is more important; (2) since tastes of copydesk

chiefs vary, the headwriter has to be alert to the dictums and prejudices of his boss.

In the American fashion, headlines "give the story away" so the
skimmer can decide what he wants to read in detail. But "feature
heads," another whole category of headlines, give only a hint of the
story. In magazines, of course, these are simply "titles." Such heads
do not summarize but rather try to capture interest. They may lack
verbs or subjects, as sometimes mere fragments arouse the reader's
curiosity.

Traditional headlines usually go on spot news stories. Feature-
head treatment best fits material like the human-interest story or the
personality sketch. It may pun. It may twist a common phrase or
aphorism. It may employ alliteration. As we said earlier, such heads
require an imaginative or witty deskman. He can also apply his talent to the occasional straight news story when a traditional summary head doesn't provide insight into the story. A clever, catchy
head may do the job. Some editors, to describe this situation, have a
slogan: "If you can't tell it, sell it."

"Almost anything goes" is the motto for the writer of feature
heads. But copydesk traditions are quite firm about news headlines.
The beginning copyeditor has to have the rules firmly in mind before
he can decide which ones may be broken safely.

Creating the headline

The previous discussion suggests the two cardinal rules of the
news headline:

Cardinal rules

1. State (or imply) a complete sentence in the present tense.
2. Eliminate all articles and most adverbs and adjectives.

The first rule notes that to imply a complete sentence, as with an
infinitive or an understood verb, is permissible:

Chancellor to Speak　　　　　**Guerrillas' Goal**
At Senior Dinner　　　　　　**Victory by April**

Usually the subject of the sentence is vital to a headline, but sometimes the alert slot man will accept a head that clearly implies the
subject. Here are borderline examples:

Discusses GOP　　　　　　**Enjoins Strike**
Industrial Plan　　　　　　**In Second Day**

Beware of heads that seem to command action from the reader. This
one sounds like a plea rather than a report:

Hit Democrats'
Housing Proposal

Some editors, to whom such headlines are anathema, suggest that
too much permissiveness may lead to the ridiculous:

Beat Grandma
And 3 Babies

The second rule, banning articles, also has exceptions. Sometimes a head reads and fits better with an article:

Judge Charges Teen-agers
'On the Loose' at Night

Major rules

Beyond these two cardinal rules lie five other guidelines for head-writing. Most of them stem from our discussion of good and bad heads and are given here more or less in descending order of importance.

Be accurate. If necessary, sacrifice color and drama in a headline to avoid leaving an erroneous impression.

Accuracy may force the copyeditor to sift the story for the kernel of the news. Of course if the lead is buried, the good copyeditor revises the story so the major news at the top then draws the head from the revised lead. But an interpretive news story may properly start with a less pointed lead than a spot news story; then the head-writer has to grasp the full meaning of the story and try to summarize that accurately.

Here, for example, is the lead of a story in the *New York Times*:

ALBANY, April 24—Evidence that the Legislature is embroiled in its adjournment rush is visible and audible this week.

Absent members are being voted "aye" by the leadership to pass favored bills. Legislators cannot get copies of bills even as the bills are being passed, lobbying is rampant and many legislators have dropped all pretense of parliamentary politeness and are literally snarling at each other....

The *Times* copyeditor summarized the whole piece with this head:

Tension Rises as Windup Nears at Albany

Be specific and concrete. "One-eyed thief" is better than "robber" or "man"; "3,000 bales" is better than "cotton." One of the problems in the above illustrations about an interracial housing bill was to be more specific than just "bill." A major headline problem of recent years has been the need to boil complicated civil rights movements and actions down into a single headline word such as "rights." Vague, abstract words make headlines without punch. But blunt words which fit may bias.

Use strong verbs. Avoid jelly words like "discuss" and "indicate" and forms of "to be." As in good news story style, use strong verbs in the active voice—*slash, pinpoint, reveal, assail, hit, kill.* Some otherwise good words have been used so much that good editors avoid or ban their use; these include *rap, sift, probe* and *flay.* Remember that verbs must be accurate as well as active. So perhaps *assail* should be replaced by *criticize*, or *denounce* by *chide*.

Start with the news. The first line of the head should tell the reader what he wants to know immediately. A short noun followed by a short, active verb will usually do:

Pope Decries ...

Teachers Revolt ...

U.S. Shifts Lead ...

Of the five w's used in the lead, the top line of the head summarizes the *who* and *what*.

But sometimes the body acting is less important and newsworthy, at least in a label-word, than is the body acted upon. So, as indicated already, "congress" and "legislature" as the first word of a head probably will have less pulling power than the tag for the legislation passed, as for example *pollution bill* or *teen draft act*. Though such a subject forces the verb into the weaker passive form, strength can still be given, as with *debated, argued,* or *killed.*

Punctuate correctly. Some beginning headwriters mistakenly cut out punctuation marks as well as articles. As figure 4-7 shows, punctuation is the same in heads as other copy, except that the period almost never ends a headline. Commas are often necessary, as in other writing. Semicolons join independent clauses, but a semicolon in the middle of a line splits the reader's attention. To save space and improve appearance, single quotation marks may replace the traditional double ones. The dash has many good head uses, but since words are not split at the end of the line in the heads of the well-edited paper, hyphens appear only between words.

Whether periods mark a head abbreviation is a question of the paper's style; it may be Y.M.C.A. or it may be YMCA. Sometimes a paper will use periods in one group of initials but not in another, according to a tradition which the desk man must learn. Similarly, abbreviation is according to style. *Prof.* without the name, *yr.,* and *Dept.* are typical abbreviations that many newspapers would ban. But *Dr.* and *Rev.* and *Co.* (with appropriate names) or *Pct.* or *U.N.,* would be used without hesitation. Nicknames, like "Rocky" or "Ronnie," as well as first names alone or initials only—like "LBJ," "Spiro," and "Ted"—are taboo on some papers though frequently used by others.

Shot by police, wounded youth faces charge

Fig. 3-7. Punctuating headlines. Punctuation, as in these heads, follows the conventions of English sentences, without the ending period.

Mrs. Dittler, 97, Dies in Hospital; Services Monday

SMITH SEES TALKS NEAR 'A CLIMAX'

Jersey Will Spend $30-Million on Rails

All sorts of other traditions and preconceptions hedge the major rules. One paper may avoid the verb "eye" in heads; another will use names of only the most prominent personages in headlines. But all agree that numerals may be used in heads, even to begin a line. (See fig. 4-7.)

Minor rules Most editors would further agree on these five minor rules:

Don't split. "Splitting" a head means dividing a natural grouping of words by the end of a line. The most heinous split puts the "to" of an infinitive at the end of one line and the verb on the next:

Mayor Promises to
Study Rent Frauds

Splitting prepositional phrases is almost as bad. But it is also poor practice to sever "have" or "will" from the rest of the verb, or separate an adjective from the noun it modifies. (To keep headline writers sane, editors usually allow splits in decks or between the second and third lines of a three-line head.)

Don't repeat. A good headline, like a good sentence, avoids simple-minded repetition. **Fair Manager Tells Plans for Fair** obviously is awkward. Copyeditors also should eschew awkward repetition of sounds, as in **Legislators Eye New Racing Legislation**.

One of the greatest temptations is to repeat a word from the head in the deck. Even use of a synonym sounds strained, so the deck should usually reveal a second angle.

The subject of the top head may be implied in a deck that starts with a verb. If the subject is omitted in the top, however, it must begin the deck. The following head is wrong because "investigators," not "wild animals," is the subject of "charge":

Charge Cages
Old, Filthy

Wild Animals in Deplorable
Condition, Say Investigators

This head properly handles the omission of subject:

Probers Charge
Zoo Coops Filthy

Claim Wild Animals
'In Deplorable Condition'

Don't overpack. It is good advice to try to get many ideas into a head; good practice avoids padding and thinning. Yet one can cross a line where the head becomes so packed with ideas that the reader has trouble translating it. One of the greatest dangers is in piling up nouns as modifiers. **State police investigators** is clear to most. **State police traffic toll investigators** is more difficult, but **State police major highway traffic toll investigators** is impossible.

Don't use headlinese. Good English is best. As indicated already, headlinese is the language of overworked words. They may be the short, punchy verbs, so some editors object to even *hit* and *gut* as headlinese. Certain nouns, such as *cops* and *tryst*, are overworked and slangy. Stay alert to usage; when a word becomes a cliché, avoid it.

Homely words become headlinese when used for their size and not their sense. One of the most infelicitous such uses is "said" for "termed," "called," or "described as." Those who employ this poor English can argue that it is short for "is said to be," but the mind boggles at fitting in the missing words, as in this head from an Eastern paper:

**Red Bloc
Trade Said
Beneficial**

Called counts only one and one-half characters more than *said* and in this instance would have fit. (Words like *called* or *labeled* are considered attributive words. They indicate to the reader that someone is making a statement. Without such words the headline would become a flat statement, like **Red Bloc Trade Beneficial**, which would be an *editorial* head appropriate on the editorial page but not over news stories.)

Don't be ambiguous. Mushy words leave mushy meanings. The many legitimate meanings of a single English word make the writer's job difficult. The verb *will*, in faulty context, may appear to be a noun, which one reader may mistake for "determination," another for "legal document," or vice versa. Humor sometimes results from unexpected double meanings.

**Roberts Will Suit
Stalls over Horses**

Precision is essential in heads, as illustrated by earlier discussion of Governor Rockefeller's reaction to "bow."

Making heads fit

Fitting the letters of a head to a given space is simply a question of figuring out how many of a certain size will go into a line and choosing words with no more than that number.

In the long single line of six or eight columns, this is easy. Here one quickly determines (perhaps by counting heads in old papers) that he can get so many letters in; usually it is thirty-five to forty-five or more, and this means he has six to ten words. He adds, drops, and changes words until he comes out with about the right total. There are enough spaces between words that the printer can fill in with unobtrusive space if the line is a little short.

The problem becomes more difficult when the head must fit the space of only a column or two. The reason is not only that there is room for fewer letters but that letters vary in width; a short space increases the importance of those variations.

Most of the small letters do not vary much in width, of course. So they are simply counted as one character or unit. Some letters are wider, and regardless of the exact variation, this greater width is figured out at 50 percent for counting purposes. The small *m*, for example, is counted as 1-1/2 units, half again as big as an *a* or *b*. On the other hand, some narrow letters—such as *i*—count 1/2. Most punctuation marks also count 1/2.

Capital letters, of course, are generally wider. In the cap-and-lower head which predominates today, therefore, the basic count is 1-1/2 units for most capitals. The wide ones, *M* and *W*, count as 2, and the narrow ones, *I* and *J*, are 1.

A space must of course be allowed between words. It may be counted 1/2. Some copyeditors like to count space between words as 1 because they then feel able to crowd more letters in, since the typesetter can then use less than a full unit of space. But for a tight count, 1/2 is acceptable.

Here is a table for quick reference which shows "the counts" for the characters in a typical case of type:

Lowercase Letters	*Count*
All except f, i, l, m, t and w	1
f, i, l, t (remembered easily by lumping the four letters into the word lift)*	1/2
m and w	1-1/2
Uppercase Letters	
All except I, J, M and W	1-1/2
I and J	1
M and W	2
Miscellaneous	
&	1-1/2
All figures except 1	1
$ % ? " #	1
1 and . , - : ; ! ' ( )	1/2
Space between words	1/2

The counts in this table will work for most head types used by newspapers. The copyeditor new to a paper will find out quickly whether it applies to the faces used there. The *t* may have to be counted 1 rather than 1/2, since it runs wider in some faces. The miscellaneous symbols such as the dollar sign and ampersand may vary from the count given; but they appear in a small minority of heads, and adjustment can be made when they do. Some changes may be made in the table to fit the fonts in use, and other quirks of individual faces can be kept in mind. The *Syracuse Post-Standard*, for example, uses one sans serif type with a very narrow *J* and *r*, so heads which count a shade over the maximum will sometimes, in fact, fit.

* In some faces *j* also counts 1/2.

Note in these lines how the width of the letters actually varies, in spite of identical counts:

MWQ	IJS	mwq	fijlt	Bodoni
MWQ	IJS	mwq	fijlt	New Times Roman
MWQ	IJS	mwq	fijlt	Univers

Awareness of such shades of difference may help a copyeditor, pushed against a deadline, to decide to send a tight head to the composing room with a minimum of fear it will have to be sent back to him for rewriting.

Copyeditors work out their own schemes for rapid counting. Take, for example, this head, used by a Western daily:

Drug Offers
Leprosy Hope

The letters of the first line count this way:

$$D \quad r \quad u \quad g \qquad O \quad f \quad f \quad e \quad r \quad s$$

$$1\tfrac{1}{2} \quad 1 \quad 1 \quad 1 \quad \tfrac{1}{2} \quad 1\tfrac{1}{2} \quad \tfrac{1}{2} \quad \tfrac{1}{2} \quad 1 \quad 1 \quad 1$$

The beginner will probably count this simply by adding one number at a time: "1-1/2, 2-1/2, 3-1/2, 4-1/2, 5, 6-1/2, 7, 7-1/2, 8-1/2, 9-1/2, and 10-1/2." But the experienced man knows that a space followed by an ordinary capital counts 2. Two f's can be grouped as 1.

$$D \quad r \quad u \quad g, \qquad O \quad f \quad f \quad e \quad r \quad s$$

$$1\tfrac{1}{2} \quad 1 \quad 1 \quad 1 \quad 2 \qquad 1 \qquad 1 \quad 1 \quad 1$$

So he can count more rapidly: 1-1/2, 2-1/2, 3-1/2, 4-1/2, 6-1/2, 7-1/2 plus 3 (*e, r,* and *s*), or 10-1/2. Another way is to count all the letters and spaces as one: 11. If the count available is 12 or 13, no further counting is necessary. But for precision, a copyeditor can take the 11, add 1/2 for the capital *D* and subtract 1 for the *f*'s, and he gets the correct answer, 10-1/2.

To mutter "1-1/2, 2, 3-1/2, 4-1/2. . ." or to make all kinds of marks above or below a head wastes time. It is much quicker to count everything as 1 and then make the adjustments required by the thin or fat letters. In many cases he will note that a fat letter will balance a thin one, leaving the count unchanged. Beginners should learn to count at least by twos and even by fives. "Drug Offers" he can look at and count 5 ("drug" plus a space), 10 (adding "offer"), and 11 at the last letter.

Also, since many names are in the news often, he should glance at the name and know what the count is. For example, "Nixon" and "Kennedy"are frequently in headlines. One counts 5, and the other 7. By adding a count for the space, the editor can add 6 to the rest of a "Nixon head" and 8 to the rest of a "Kennedy head."

The count we have been discussing so far applies to heads that mix caps and lowers. All-cap heads are harder to read but easier to count. The papers that still use them use a different counting system.

An easy rule is: all capital letters except four count 1; *M* and *W* are now 1-1/2, and *I* and *J* are 1/2. Punctuation marks also have varied counts, though most marks are 1/2.

Making heads attractive

Graphically, the phrases of a headline are lines put together in simple designs. Obviously these designs should be chosen to please the eye. Similarity of type is important. For example, lines of very large and very small type clash. The two or three lines of a deck all should be of similar lengths. In the stepped head, for example, lines that vary no more than a unit or two will create the symmetrical design on the left rather than the unbalanced example on the right:

```
    XXXXXXXXXXXX           XXXXXXXX
    XXXXXXXXXXXX           XXXXXXXXXXXXXXX
     XXXXXXXXXXXX             XXXXXX
```

The flush-left head was invented to overcome the problems of writing the lines to very nearly the same length, and it is true that attractive heads can be written where the lines in these heads vary three or even four units. Some papers permit more. However, too great a variation makes a flush-left head ugly too. Compare the attractiveness of these two examples:

```
    XXXXXXXXXX            XXXXXXXX
    XXXXXXXXXXXXXX        XXXXXXXXXXXXXX
    XXXXXXXXXXXX          XXXX
```

Some editors argue that the all-cap line is more attractive than the caps-and-lower because the full-height letters create a clean, straight line on both top and bottom. Most papers still use some all-cap headlines, but they favor mixed upper and lower case letters for legibility because we are accustomed to seeing them mixed in all our reading. To maximize readability the usual practice is to capitalize first words of lines and all other words except articles and prepositions. Admittedly, such lines are ragged on top. Several recently redesigned papers have gone to a head which is mostly lower-case. Whether this very readable style of head is more attractive, because streamlined, than the more traditional kinds is a matter of taste.

While the simple, flush-left head is by all odds the most popular today, newspapers are not completely standardized in the United States. Heads can be pyramids, inverted pyramids, or centered styles. Headwriters, like magazine editors, also create special forms, especially on feature materials. The full-box head is no longer very popular, but the three-quarter box is occasionally used. Sometimes double or shaded rules (Ben Day) are used instead of simply hairlines or one-point rules; frequently words are inserted into the top rule, kicker-fashion. (See fig. 4-8 for examples of box rules and unusual headline shapes.)

In addition to rules and boxes, black-and-white designs or shaded illustrations are often part of standing heads. (See fig. 4-9.) Usually these heads run the same day after day. But space requirements shift, and to adjust a permanent heading a copyeditor must know the type used. The *Rochester Times-Union*, for example, has a daily feature made up of short personality items. Under a three-sided box which may be three or more columns wide is the word "People" in 42 Ultra Bodoni. Each day there is a new 18-point Bodoni head alongside this word, two lines inverted-pyramid style.

Fig. 3-8. Boxed heads. Rules are used in a number of ways to dress up heads, with the three-sided or three-quarter box especially popular for leading the eye into the story. Note the kickers cut into top rules and the varied headline shapes. (The deck of the **Wall Street Journal** head (right) is a hanging indention, a shape now rare on American newspaper pages.)

The Hello Business:
Welcomers Abound
For Moving Families
• • •
But Business, Not Friendship,
Spurs the Visits by Women;
Bargaining With the Milkman

Report on Cigarettes
Some Filters Are Branded
Worse than the Non-Filters

Hijack Plane
18 Invaders
Try to Claim
The Falklands

NEW TESTAMENT
EDITION PUT IN
SIMPLE ENGLISH

Labor Council
Stays Neutral
On Governor

Background
Young Red 'Front'
THE W.E.B. DuBois Club was founded on the West
Coast in June, 1964, to succeed the Young Communist

Fig. 3-9. Standing heads. Regularly used headings, often with a cut, are kept ready for quick insertion. The bottom ones here guide readers inside. Note that the simple, clean, uncrowded heads are the most atttractive.

ON THE SCENE . . .
In Louisville

Good
Morning

News Digest   Sunny and Cool

From the bookshelf
Dropping in on the Indians . . . . By Rhea Jane

Easy-to-find . . . Easy-to-read
INSIDE YOUR TIMES-UNION
MAVERICK MILLIONAIRE hurls political
charges.   Page 9A

POST GUIDE to top stories
VIETNAM VICTORY   " . . . Just stand by
PREDICTIONS
DEPARTMENT

Since each paper has its own system for preparing heads and sending them properly marked to the composing room, the new copyeditor has to inquire about local rules. However, certain procedures are the same for all papers.

Heads may be written at the top of copy or on a separate piece of paper, but a newspaper's procedure generally calls for writing the head on the story if the type is small. This is why the reporter has been instructed to start typing his story a third or a half of the way down the first page. If the copyeditor can quickly write the simple head above it, then the compositor can, without changing typesetting machines, set the head at the same time he sets the story. For example, the smallest head on most papers is a single line of the body type set in bold face. It would be foolish to put such a head on a separate piece of paper and make the printers assemble head and story from separate galleys.

Nevertheless, many heads cannot be set on the machine which sets the story. On papers with limited facilities a printer may have to set the big heads by hand; typically, however, a machine specially suited for casting big sizes of type will be used. Either way, the copyeditor must prepare some heads for such necessities.

It is conceivable that, on a slow operation, the stories could all be set and then passed on for the heads all to be set. But it is clearly much faster and more efficient to have men working on the stories and the heads at the same time. For bigger heads, therefore, the copy desk typically writes out the head on a separate sheet of paper. A key word, or *slug*, is given to the story, and this same slug is put on the paper with the head. Finding these slugs in the galleys of type, the printer can assemble the proper head with each story. (The slug line is then thrown into the discard, or *hellbox*, since it has served its communication purpose.)

Aside from the slug, the other main communication to the printer is of course about the style and size of type. Where there is a headline schedule, this information is generally given simply as the head number. For example, a copyeditor might jot "Astro" and "#2" on a story about astronauts. He would write the same coding on the paper with the Number 2 astronaut head he has created. (See fig. 4-10.) The slug on both story and head would then look like this in the proof:

$$A_{STRO} \#2$$

Some papers, particularly smaller ones, do not use the slug system to identify copy. They use guidelines, which are the first word or two of the headline itself. For one-edition papers the guideline saves a little time, because the slug does not have to be set on each headline. The Astro story, for example, could have been slugged MOON, CAPSULE, HEIGHT or anything else. But in the guideline system the word ASTRONAUTS would have to be marked on the top of the copy. Note the differences:

Slug system:

(handwritten) ASTRO · 2 | Astronauts Soar To Record Heights

Guideline system:

(handwritten) 2 | Astronauts Soar To Record Heights

When the copyeditor goes beyond the head schedule to create other headings, he must give concise but clear instructions to the printer. If he wants a single, centered line of 24-point Ultra Bodoni, he may write:

(handwritten) 24 Ultra Bod. cent.

For two lines of 30-point Cheltenham, flush left, capitals and lower case, in a box made of rules, he may write:

(handwritten) 30 Chelt. fl. left c&lc = 3 col. box

or even more simply:

(handwritten) 30 Chelt | Astronauts Soar To Record Heights

The headwriter can quickly learn the shorthand of different shops. "Ultra" may be enough without "Bod." or "B" because the printer knows that the only "ultra" type used is Bodoni.

The application of the rules and guidelines may be demonstrated with the handling of an illustrative story. The slot man marks "C" at the top of copy which begins with this lead:

Writing a headline

WASHINGTON—Ardent civil rights backers in Congress are anxiously watching a sharp change in the mood and temper of White America. . . .

The story goes on to point up several recent news items which indicate a turn against further desegregation.

The copyeditor checks the head schedule, unless he has it memorized, to find the requirements of a C head: three flush-left lines with a maximum count of 13-1/2. Mentally he skeletonizes the lead into headline form: "Civil rights backers watch sharp change in mood." But he can be more specific if he notes the direction of the change, so he reframes the last idea as "sharp dip in desegregation zeal" or "sharp rise in resistance to integration." The words are long for the low count, but he can begin:

Civil Rights Backers
Watch Sharp Dip
In Desegregation Zeal

These lines count 18, 15, and 19-1/2—all too long. "In" can be moved up to the second line (creating a split), but the third line remains 3-1/2 counts too long. How about making it "Integration Zeal"? Fourteen, but it might be squeezed in. "Zeal to Change" is only 13 and would be sharper.

The headwriter has to trim, tighten, and re-arrange. If he drops "Civil" in the first line, it fits nicely. The second line can be made to fit by eliminating "Sharp" and by finding a way to get rid of the wide W (dips are not watched anyway); so it becomes "Note Dip in" —a bit short, but acceptable. When "Drop" is substituted for "Dip," the head becomes:

Rights Backers
Note Drop in
Zeal to Change

This does the job. But let's say that the slot man wants to get in the idea of "growing resistance" and tosses it back for rewriting. The second line can then become "Note Rise in"—but in what? "Integration Resistance" is much too long and difficult. "Mood to Resist"? That fits, and the head is now:

Rights Backers
Note Rise in
Mood to Resist

This lacks the tone of sharpness which the story attributes to the rise. Some editors would prefer "zoom" to "rise," which fills that second line out a bit anyway; but others would think "zoom" smacks too much of the sports or financial pages. (See fig. 4-10.)

(A metropolitan newspaper which used this story carried this two-column head:

Civil rights
backers note
mood change

The lines fill nicely, though the direction of the change has to be inferred by the reader from his knowledge of recent events. Note the capitalization style.)

Illustrations can be misleading because they may imply that the creative process is absolutely straightforward. Some headlines come easily and naturally and fit the first time, but often a copyeditor has to ponder several possibilities. He should try to put the whole head together at once and make space adjustments afterward. If he tinkers to make the first line perfect before going on to the rest, he will likely find it impossible to fit other lines to the first line.

Flexibility is most important. The copyeditor should try not to get his mind "locked in" on a particular wording. If a pet phrase doesn't work after a bit of trying, he should stop wasting time with it and use a new approach. He may have to abandon the key statement of the lead and rethink what the story is trying to say.

Here are three pointers on the knack of writing heads, probably in the order the copyeditor will use them.

Developing the knack

Three pointers

Try for good short synonyms when the head doesn't fit. Since English has many short verbs, these can probably be juggled more easily than others: e.g., *criticizes, assails, slaps, raps, quits.* Sometimes a slight loss in clarity is unavoidable when substituting, as when "School Superintendent" becomes "School Chief." Initials and nicknames can be used, though good desk procedure requires that they be immediately clear to readers and that they not become too numerous. (Such means may be the only feasible way to distinguish among news figures with the same name; in a city with a mayor named Rudolph Hammerhill, headwriters would use "Rudy," "Ham," "Mayor," and other such codes to communicate the right name quickly.)

Fig. 3-10. Writing a head. The final step in writing the civil rights headline discussed in the text is putting it on copy paper. The example shows the head slugged and marked for a "C" head on the printer's head-schedule.

Reverse the head if the first subject-verb pattern doesn't fit.

**Rogers Sees
Venezuela Revolt**

will fit if changed to

**Venezuelan Revolt
Seen by Rogers**

Look for a new angle. In the integration example above, it might have become necessary to try something about Congress pondering news of race developments.

Decks and kickers

To get a little more display than a single two- or three-line head will give, editors sometimes use headlines made up of two decks. A banner headline clearly needs one, two or even more decks to lead into the story. See fig. 4-11.

Television's Trials
TV Industry Is Feeling
Government Pressure,
But the Money Rolls In

Fairness of News Questioned,
Cigaret Ads Face Banning,
Licenses Are in Jeopardy

Station Prices, Profits Rise

CHANGE ON SCHOOL LEVY

Missouri House Approves Proposed Change in Constitution to Aid in
Raising Funds—Approval by Voters Is Required
Before It Goes Into Effect

WELFARE NOD

Program Clears Legisla-
ture, Goes to Governor
for Signature

AN EMERGENCY CLAUSE

Tax and Budget Bills
Must Be Acted on
Before Midnight

Bulletins

Fig. 3-11. Two or more decks. The subordinate unit of the typical two-part head, often called simply "the deck," comes in varied styles and shapes. Though the popularity of heads with several decks has declined over the last generation or two, a few papers still use them.

Traditionally, the lower deck of an ordinary single-column head is two or three lines in inverted pyramid style:

```
xxxxxxxxxxxxxxxxxxxx
xxxxxxxxxxxx
xxxxx
```

Graphically, it is important in the three-line deck to have the lines step in evenly, as in the step head. Head schedules give counts for the full column width, and the top line is written to fill; simply counting letters is usually satisfactory with deck sizes and counts. If the top line is 32, the full count, the second line might be 24 to 26, and the third line should then be 16 to 18. Or the second line could be 20 and the third line 8 to 10. If either the second or third line is too long or too short to provide even steps, the head will be ugly.

Content, of course, is an even more important consideration in the second deck. It should not merely repeat the top. The deck should point up or develop a new angle. The rules for keeping it active and compact are the same as for top decks.

Care should be taken that the headline reads clearly when read straight through. The lower deck may begin with a verb, but the subject then is understood to be the same as that of the top. In figure 4-12 "Mrs. Gandhi" is the subject not only of the top but of the lower deck. A shift to "Gets Offer of Unrestricted . . ." with "Pakistan" intended as subject would be a blooper of the same genre as a dangling participle.

MRS. GANDHI ASKS PAKISTAN'S AMITY

Offers Unrestricted Travel and Economic Cooperation

Special to The New York Times
NEW DELHI, Sept. 4—Prime Minister Indira Gandhi tonight offered "economic cooperation" with Pakistan.
In a "person to person" talk, broadcast over the All-India Radio, Mrs. Gandhi also renewed India's pledge "to abjure the use of force in the settlement of differences" between the two nations.
Her conciliatory offer came 'ter a period of mounting ten- 'between the two countries. nt weeks they have ac- 'h other of massive '4-ups on the bor- 'hensions

Fig. 3-12. Subject of deck. Space can be saved by using the subject of the main head as subject of the deck; here, it is understood, Mrs. Gandhi "offers."

A less common form of deck—the hanging indention—is somewhat easier to write than the inverted pyramid:

xxxxxxxxxxxxxxxxxxxx
xxxxxxxxxxxxxxxx
xxxxxx

The top line fills, and the second line should be two or three characters shorter. The third line then can vary all the way from a few letters to the same length as the second and still be attractive. Otherwise, rules for the pyramid deck apply to this deck.

Since mid-century, the most popular lower deck by far has been the brief, flush-left head. Usually it is two lines, with the right side ragged. Though the number of words available is usually much more limited than in the old-style, inverted-pyramid deck, the content rules are the same for both; the editor constructs it just as he constructs the flush-left head. (See fig. 4-13.)

Fig. 3-13. Popular deck styles. These examples show the popular styles of decks for single-column heads. Pyramid, once the most popular, is now less frequently used than flush-left.

'Hidden'
jobless
on rise
▽   ▽
*Rate upsets
labor office*

Blast Kills
3 at Toledo
Steel Plant

500 Flee Plant
As Fire Roars

Cost of Living
Up Sharply
During July

Automatic Pay Rises
Increase Concern
Of Administration

SAYS SCHOOLS NOT
FOR SOCIAL CHANGE

Dallas, Tex., Educator Warns
Against Using Them as
Welfare Agency

DISABLED
JET AVERTS
SEA CRASH

Bound For Canada,
DC-8 Lands Safely
In Ireland

Another subordinate head is the kicker, whose growing popularity was indicated above. Almost all newspapers now use this device of a little head above the main head, though research shows that kickers are seldom read. They do, however, provide a ribbon of white space above the head and thus help attract attention. So they should be kept short, to maximize the white space, and their wording should stir interest with a new angle or touch. The words that would make a good, crisp flush-left second deck probably also will make a good kicker, but it should be a little more striking or dazzling than the typical deck. Sometimes dropping the verb will do the trick, for labels are more readily accepted in kickers. A conservative kicker looks like a regular head:

Detectives Spot New Evidence

But a kicker can deliver more punch:

Mysterious Time Bomb

A quote draws attention to the main head:

'I Was Framed!'

To emphasize that not all news is bad, the *Denver Post* regularly employs a little all-cap kicker, "GOOD NEWS," sometimes in red. Papers also use kickers to indicate columns or regular features. (See fig. 4-14.)

ALL'S QUIET
A Feeling Of Relief In Cicero

GOOD NEWS TODAY
CU Receives $674,000 Grant

MOVIES
Suspenseful Terror Stalks Murder Yarn

OIL MAY HAVE COME FROM SHIP
Mystery Goo Hits Beaches

Theories crack
Market antics still puzzling

Fig. 3-14. Kickers. Typically underlined, the kicker is now widely used by many papers and often replaces the deck. It may give more information in verb–head form or simply add a word or two of identification. Though the type face of the kicker may virtually match the head or be markedly different, it usually represents a shift to italic or caps.

As the flush-left head and kicker have flourished, the crossline has virtually died out. This headline element is a single column-wide line, typically in caps, that appears with four or more decks, usually sandwiched between two inverted pyramids. Copyeditors on the few papers which use crosslines can quickly pick up their rules, but it may be generalized that this form summarizes a new angle with a present-tense verb, just as other subordinate decks do.

One form of head, widely used both yesterday and today, is the *subhead*. Ordinarily it is simply two or three words of boldface, the same size as the body type, in the body of a story.

There are two schools of thought about handling the body of a story. One group of editors wants to break it into short "takes" with subheads every three or four paragraphs. The paragraphs not next to subheads may be set boldface and indented. The other school contends that such typographic devices tend to make stories harder rather than easier to read. These editors advocate long, unbroken stretches of body type, with few subheads. The spread of TTS and of horizontal makeup patterns, which reduce the amount of unbroken gray body type, supports the second school. Many papers, of course, will choose a middle ground and use a moderate number of subheads.

Rules for the subhead are much the same as for major heads—present tense, no articles, active voice, and so on. Some papers permit a simple label of two words, because their primary concern is to break up type. Research shows their major practical value is this graphic purpose; still, at least for a minority, well-written subheads can help a reader find parts of a story that stimulate him to read the whole piece.

Except on rare occasions, the subhead should refer to the paragraph immediately following. Few things frustrate a careful reader more than to have curiosity piqued by a good subhead and then have to search down two or three paragraphs to find this angle.

The copyeditor usually writes the subhead right in the copy at the appropriate place. He then marks the margin "sub" or "ffclc" (full face caps and lower case) or simply "BF" (boldface). He may use brackets to indicate centering, but printers usually follow subhead style unless directed otherwise. (See fig. 4-15.)

Subheads and jumpheads

The declaration contained, apart from the pledge by the two countries to abjure force, various steps toward normalizing their relations.

Peoples Kept Apart

However, except for the withdrawal of troops to positions held before fighting broke out and an exchange of ambassadors, there has been no other significant progress. The peoples of the two nations still live

countries to abjure force, various steps toward normalizing their relations. *Peoples Kept Apart*

However, except for the withdrawal of troops to positions held before fighting broke out and an exchange of

Fig. 3-15. Subheads. The typical subhead is written into copy this way. A designation such as "BF" or "ffclc" may be used instead of "sub" to indicate boldface is to be used. Illustration also shows how this subhead in the **Times** story on Mrs. Gandhi (cf. fig. 4-12) appears in print.

As type sizes have increased, subheads have grown bolder. Some stories, especially in wide measures, may be broken up with two-line flush-left heads in 12-, 14-, or even 18-point bold italic.

Dingbats—typographic designs such as round dots (bullets) or stars—sometimes accompany a subhead. White space is another important break-up element—around subheads, with dingbats, and sometimes simply by itself. These attention-getters should be used with restraint, for too many will annoy rather than attract the reader.

A number of papers make the first two or three words of a paragraph boldface caps with a break of white space or three bold dots and space just above this paragraph. (See fig. 4-16.) A few papers, in special sections, use the magazine-style printing device of *initial letter* to kick-off major feature stories. This device is a beginning capital several points bigger than the text type and may even be used to start paragraphs in the body of articles, especially on editorial pages.

State Department and White House.
Weary of Work Going for Nought
The arrangement has been zealously adhered to by the President. There has been no break over a fundamental policy issue. Goldberg,

accept offers of help in crossing the border.
* * *
One Cuban woman recalled her stay in Mexico City with

descent in the area. Most speak Russian.

Sister Ships at Dock

The Fedor Litke and the Alexy Chirikov are 300-foot sister ships built to

mountaineers, will name nine men.
To Write Constitution
The assembly will be charged with turning out a

said the revolutionary teenagers are under direct control of the Mao-Lin faction.
PAPERS BACK DRIVE
It went on to say that "until very recently 'anti-Mao ele-

tion already taken has moderated the growth of bank credit.
ACTION EXPLAINED
"However, in view of increasing pressures on prices stem-

would have to be amended to permit the high-rise buildings on the waterfront.
● Jack V. McKenzie, former data processing man-

learned to listen to the strident voices.

NOR DID HE ever manage to convince the black community that he was con-

of advances would be kept to narrow bounds.

THE STRONG performance of blue chips was cited as one of the reasons why

moves with real estate dealers prove unsuccessful.
● ● ●
KING SCHEDULED a strategy meeting for tonight to evaluate today's activities and

Fig. 3-16. Subhead styles. While the typical subhead is probably still boldface caps and lowers, centered, newspapers use many other devices to break up copy, as illustrated. Some papers are dropping subheads. But where they do, copyeditors must be sure to use horizontal make-up to keep the strips of type short, or to work out other methods to prevent the columns from looking gray, old-fashioned, and forbidding. Note in the bottom row how the importance of division increases, left to right, by the addition of boldface, space, and dingbats.

Stories continued inside the paper need some heading for the continuation, or *jump*. Formerly the *jump head* was the front page head, or very like it. Modifying this tradition, some papers now use a smaller head for the jump. It typically has a "better count" than the one on the front page, and the copyeditor may be able to get ideas and precision here which he abandoned in writing the major head. (A reverse-plate "logo"—white letters on a dark gray background—sometimes helps the eye spot the jump.)

The jump word is often a single key word. It may be employed with a jump head, but more often it stands alone. Like the slug, this word should distinguish the story from all others that day. The jump word is set in larger type or caps; and a box, rules, or white space should make it easy to spot. (See fig. 4-17.)

Fig. 3-17. Jumps. Editors have developed ingenious heading devices for inside pages to help readers find continued stories. Regular heads are often used to emphasize the news content of these pages. Many editors also use a gimmick, such as a reverse plate, so that the reader's searching eye can spot the jump quickly. A slug word, perhaps with rules, is especially attention-getting, as illustrated by the two bottom rows.

This discussion of headlines has moved from theory to the nuts and bolts of head counts and then to the lowly subhead and jump head. A copyeditor may similarly leave broad principle behind and become involved in the minutiae of quick writing and fast counts— "anything that fits." Professional editing, however, keeps to the high purpose of the newspaper. Even though a head must fit a space and flag attention, its main purpose is to inform quickly and truthfully. And the best headwriter produces such accurate heads so regularly that applying his ethics becomes as habitual and automatic as counting *m* as 1-1/2.

4 Printing: past, present, future

A girl fresh out of journalism school took a job on a medium-sized daily. On her tenth working day she was told to go into the composing room to see if certain material could be printed. A printer started to give her a long, involved explanation. "Oh, I see," the girl said after a minute, "you mean you don't have the right base to make it type high." He was astounded, and she was treated as a colleague in the composing room from then on.

Like the girl, any copyeditor ought to be comfortable around most printing operations. He does not have to be an expert, but he should know how to mark copy for the compositor, how long it takes for such routine tasks of makeup as the front page, and what a printer can and cannot do. Otherwise he will mislead—and have to make corrections later. He may send so much copy to be set that the paper will appear hours late. Or he may order the impossible, and so raise the blood pressure of everyone in the composing room.

It is particularly difficult now to be current on printing because changes and innovations come so rapidly. Only an expert can keep up with the latest developments. To cope with this problem some newspapers hire experts to do little more than advise on what kind of new equipment to buy. While the copyeditor doesn't need to know the intricacies of printing machinery, he must grasp the processes his own newspaper uses and how to get the most out of them. This knowledge of familiar printing processes, together with an understanding of the paper's aims, makes an editor ready to move into responsible positions. He is able to understand and assess the advice of the expert. Editors-in-chief and publishers these days spend great chunks of their time examining new printing equipment to see if it can do a better and cheaper job for their paper. Lesser editors who understand the problems can become part of the decision-making team.

Before about 1950 understanding printing processes was relatively easy. Nearly every daily newspaper used the same principle: a raised surface pressed ink on paper—the traditional letterpress method. Stories and advertisements were typically set by a typecasting machine, the Linotype. Engravings, made by etching grooves into a zinc plate, printed pictures. As only minor changes had occurred since 1886 when Ottmar Mergenthaler invented the Linotype, a newsman who understood the basics seemsed to have a life-time knowledge of printing.

Today, however, dozens of major papers have replaced the hotmetal linecasting of the Linotype. These "set" on a strip of film or paper. And pictures may be elctronically engraved on sheets of plastic or metal. The big, heavy plates for the presses often are replaced with thin, light aluminum plates. Sometimes typesetting is automatic. Perforated tape goes to a computer which punches other tape that goes to the typesetting machine. By pushing a switch, an editor can erase part of the tape, producing in type a news story which is at least partially "edited."

Recent developments in mechanization and automation make it impossible to predict the future of newspaper printing. Perhaps today's most modern equipment will be obsolete in ten years. Perhaps a whole new concept of printing will send the equipment that dazzles so many people today to museums.

Dozens of newspapers are part way there now after purchasing electronic editing machines. Copy from wire services or reporters is put on a tape that feeds into a computer. When the copyeditor is ready to edit the story he presses a button and the story appears on what resembles a small television screen. The editor can alter the story by pressing a few buttons or by typing a few words on a keyboard. Another button sends the "copy" to the composing room by wire. Most copyeditors, unless they are resistant to change, learn to run these machines in a few days. The result of the editing, of course, is the same as though the editor were using a pencil. These machines are certain to be used widely within a few years. A Daytona Beach, Florida, editor said that his electronic editor saved him $77,000 a year. Editors and publishers are fascinated by machines that save this kind of money. They will be eager to buy such equipment. This means that the electronic invasion of the newsroom is coming swiftly and journalists will have to adjust to the innovations. An editor who is indifferent or antagonistic to the new machines will be limiting his development.

Letterpress

Letterpress is the "old-fashioned" process. The type, with raised faces like the letters on a rubber stamp, is set by a composing machine such as the Linotype, or it may (rarely) be handset. The type for stories and ads, together with relief plates for illustrations, goes into a rectangular *form* the size of the newspaper page. Ink put on the type comes off in readable form on anything pressed against it. In fact, *proofs* are simply sheets of paper pressed against forms so the type can be checked for errors.

A few weekly papers still print directly from raised type in such flat forms. Ink rolled over them transfers to sheets of newsprint which, after folding, go to the subscriber. This process is called *flat-bed printing*—because the printing is done with the form lying on a flat surface.

This process, however, entails a lot of slow and costly motion for each impression. To speed up printing, almost a century ago the concept of the wheel came into printing with the invention of the *rotary press;* innovators found a way to change the flat horizontal form into something that would rotate. Though this process requires a duplicate platemaking process called *stereotyping,* it more than makes up for that extra step in the speed of printing.

The technique is quite simple. A piece of papier-mâché, called a *matrix* or *mat* (technically a *flong*), is placed on top of the page of type. The whole thing is run through a *mat roller*, much the way wet clothes go through the wringer of an old-fashioned washing machine. The pressure exerted by the roller is intense, and the flong, squeezed hard against the type, takes on a clear, full impression of the page of type. The process thus makes the flong, or mat, into a mold. Anyone can read this mat like a newspaper; the lettering is right side up and the words read from left to right.

It has been necessary that the mat be moderately damp so it will not break under the pressure of the mat roller. Now a man called a *stereotyper* rolls the mat and puts each mat in a special oven for a minute or two to bake out the moisture. He then places it in a curved device and pours molten type metal against it. This metal, mostly lead with a little tin and antimony, hardens in a minute or two into a sturdy, curved plate that works like a big curved rubber stamp.

This *stereotype* is taken to the press and "locked" into position. A row of these plates becomes, in effect, a cylinder. As motors turn this cylinder, rollers spread ink evenly over the raised letters and illustrations. A great roll of paper, or *web*, feeding rapidly through the machine is pressed firmly against the inked surface and becomes a long roll of printed pages. These are automatically folded together in order, cut to separate each copy of the newspaper, routed to a separate room, and bundled for distribution.

Stereotypers also cast ready-made papier-mâché mats. These usually come from advertiser, but some wire service pictures, comics, crossword puzzles, and even copy come to the paper already in mat form. The stereotyper may cast these singly or paste several flat mats together before pouring molten metal over them for a *flat cast*. Such castings, cut apart if necessary, go in the ads or news columns as the flat form is made up. So they are eventually stereotyped again when the whole page goes through the mat roller.*

* Chemical companies here and abroad are attempting to improve the mat-and-metal process of stereotyping by the use of plastics. The Research Institute of the American Newspaper Publishers Association reported optimistically in 1969 on experimental use in newspaper plants of two such new methods: Letterflex, which produces flexible relief-printing plates directly from a photographic negative by etching plastic, and Hylox, which makes a stereotype matrix from plastic rather than papier-mâché.

The Linotype   Since the Linotype casts most of the type used in the letterpress process, it is important to know how it works. The machine has a set of keys much like a typewriter. When the operator taps the keys, he releases brass matrices (molds for letters) which fall into a row where together they become a single mold for a line of type.

What of spaces? The operator taps keys to insert *space bands* between words and sometimes between letters. The space band is shaped like a wedge, and the thin end goes between the words or letters. When the line of brass "mats" is full, the operator presses a lever. Almost simultaneously, the space bands are pushed upward, making the line snug. This motion *justifies* the line—spaces the letter even both right and left with previous lines. (See fig. 9-1.) The molten metal then squeezes through a slot against the line of matrices and fills the little molds; it solidifies almost instantly into a *slug*, or line of cast type.

The inventor of the Linotype also had to solve the problem of getting the brass mats back in proper order at the top of the machine in their storage place, called a *magazine*, ready to be used again.

The problem was solved by notching each mat much as a door key is notched. The A's have one pattern of notches, the B's another, etc. After the line is cast, the machine takes the used mats to the top and back of the machine where they move onto a distributor bar. Hanging by their notches they automatically ride along the bar, which is grooved in as many different patterns as there are channels to store

Fig. 4-1. Line of matrices. A matrix is a small brass mold of a letter. The composing machine assembles these matrices and the longer space-bands (used for spacing between words) in a line, as shown here. It then holds them against a mold into which molten metal is forced and so casts a slug, the metal line of type used in printing.

Fig. 4-2. Circulation of matrices. This phantom illustration shows each stage in the movement of the matrix through the Linotype machine. When keys are punched, the matrices drop into line in front of the operator, are cast (at left), and finally are redistributed to magazine (above right).

letter matrices. The A's reach a point where their notches no longer
hang onto the bar, and so drop off automatically into their channel
of the magazine. The same thing happens to the rest of the letters
and symbols so each letter rests in the proper row in the magazine—
ready to drop at the touch of its key. (See fig. 9-2.)

About 1945 many papers added an attachment to the Linotype
allowing type to be set from a perforated paper tape. The holes signaled for letters, much as an old-time player piano signaled for
notes. A person with little more than typing skill can punch the tape
by hitting letter keys on a special machine, and the tapes are then fed
into the Linotype. (See figs. 9-3 and 9-4.) This automatic typesetting
is considerably faster than the old manual way, and most letter-press
papers today use some kind of tape perforating system. As we noted
in chapter 7, most of them also use tape from the wire services to set
wire copy.

Some papers have added computers to typesetting and their
number is growing steadily. Though the computer increases efficien-
cy, it does not set type by itself. It receives one tape and produces
another. First an employee copies a story by typing on a machine
which punches tape. He simply types, using a special key for paragraph indentation, but paying no attention to justifying lines. His
tape goes into the computer, which in turn produces a tape to be fed
into a typesetting machine. The computer then justifies lines,
hyphenates words, if necessary, and even corrects some typographical errors.

Fig. 4-3. Tape perforation. As if sitting at an
ordinary typewriter, an operator runs a
Swiftape machine to perforate type, which in
turn is used in setting type.

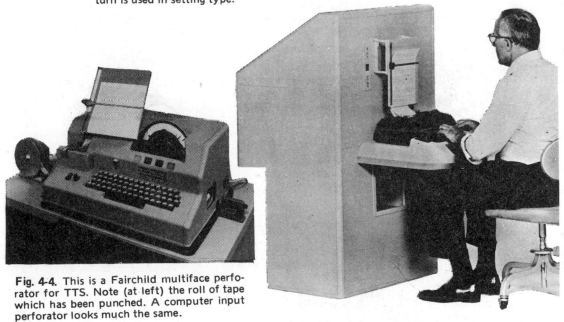

Fig. 4-4. This is a Fairchild multiface perforator for TTS. Note (at left) the roll of tape
which has been punched. A computer input
perforator looks much the same.

Art by letterpress

Pictures, collectively called *art*, are reproduced either by the conventional process of engraved metal or by an electronic method. In the conventional system acid etches hundreds of little grooves into a plate to produce an *engraving* with a pattern of minute raised dots. These print as tiny points on paper and so produce shades from dark to light. The darkest grays of the picture produce bigger black dots and smaller white areas among them; the lightest grays of course make very small dots against relatively large untouched areas. These massed points of black and white are so tiny, however, that the eye mixes them optically to form the illusion of continuous tones of gray. (See fig. 9-5.)

Fig. 4-5. Halftone screen. This picture, a corner of a large newspaper, employs a gross halftone screen. The dots are magnified for this illustration. To see how the eye blends the dot patterns used in the screens of ordinary engravings, look at the page from eight or ten feet away.

The dots are made by shooting the picture through a *screen*, which thus becomes a kind of measure in engraving. The best printing requires fine screens, which produce very tiny dots, and high quality paper. But coarser screens, with 55 or 65 lines of holes per square inch, are necessary to make cuts which will not blur ink on coarser paper. Newsprint typically requires engravings of 55-line or 65-line screen. The copyeditor ordinarily need not be concerned about screens, except to know that, should he try to introduce different ones, they will print differently, may cause disharmony, and perhaps be worse than those habitually used.

An engraving is also called a *cut*, or *zinc*, and most pictures, made up of varying shades of gray, are called *halftones*, because they are neither solid black nor solid white. When no screen is used and when all background material is removed, only certain lines remain, as for cartoons, fashion drawings, or courtroom sketches. There are, of course, no dots. These *line cuts* produce black on white, or gray if the artist has put black lines close together. (See fig. 9-6.)

Fig. 4-6. Art work. The artist is useful to the newspaper for humor and variety— and for pictures where photographers are barred. This is a line engraving, to be distinguished from a halftone (cf. fig. 9-5). Reprinted with permission of the **Los Angeles Times.**

"I wish they'd let photographers cover these trials -- court artists are sloppy!"

Electronic engraving uses either a plastic or a metal sheet. The picture fits on a drum, revolves, and an electric eye picks up varying light impulses from its varying shades. This eye controls a white-hot stylus above another drum carrying the plastic or metal. Following the shades in the picture, the stylus lightly gouges the plate to convert it to a cut (fig. 9-7). A similar machine with a V-shaped blade literally plows furrows of varying widths into a thin sheet of flexible metal. Parallel lines create the illusion of continuous gray tones.

It is difficult to stereotype the plastic cuts, so many papers simply leave room on the page plate and, with adhesive, stick the plastic to the curved metal just before the presses start to run. Since the metal plates can be stereotyped, they are more popular.

Fig. 4-7. Simple engraving. This Fairchild Scan-a-graver makes quick and inexpensive engravings. Photo or art copy put on the drum at right is engraved on the cylinder at left.

Offset

The *offset* method of printing is much different. Anyone can run his fingers over an offset printing plate and it will feel perfectly smooth. To someone raised in the letterpress tradition, this offset technique of printing from a smooth surface seems magical. Offset works, however, on the well-known principle that oil and water do not mix. So, this process provides that the parts of the offset plate meant to print will receive ink (which is basically oil) while the rest of the plate, taking only water, will reject the ink. But it must be clear that printing is *not* done directly from the offset plate. The plate transmits the image onto a press roller, which squeezes against the paper to transmit, or "offset," the printed impression.

Offset printing can use almost any kind of typesetting method. In fact, whatever can be photographed can be printed offset. This means that an offset newspaper could even be typed or handwritten and then photographed for the press plates.

This possibility has opened the door to "typesetting" methods that do not, in the traditional sense, set type at all. Most offset work uses *cold type* versus the *hot type* of letterpress, which uses the Linotype to cast molten metal. Cold type may be the output of an ordinary typewriter, of a special typewriter that allows varied spaces between words and letters, so the lines can be justified, or of other machines that turn out news stories in neat columns on a strip of film, a method commonly called *photocomposition.*

These columns of type for offset—really strips of paper or film—are pasted onto a sheet of paper the size of the newspaper page. Headlines are set on film by a separate machine and pasted onto a sheet of paper, or dummy, to produce what is called a *mechanical* or *camera copy.* The whole page is then photographed. The resulting page-sized negative is placed on a sensitized aluminum sheet resembling a cookie sheet and light is directed through the negative onto the metal for a minute or two to "burn in" the plate. The latent image of the newspaper page appears on the aluminum. A simple developing process converts the photographic image into an ink-attractive, water-repellent one. The plate, which weighs only a few ounces, then goes on the press and the press run starts.

It is possible to combine hot type with offset printing. The metal slugs are assembled in proper order and a proof is taken on quality paper. This is called a *reproduction proof* or a *repro proof.* Such proofs, pasted onto a dummy and photographed, go through the rest of the offset process. The result can be hard to distinguish from letterpress.

Offset popularity

The shift to offset by American newspapers has been rapid. The first papers to change were tiny weeklies, often with old, worn out letterpress equipment. It was easy to change over such little plants. No agreements were necessary with union printers, and personnel problems usually declined with the move. Women with typing skill could set the type. Though there are some women compositors in the letterpress method, usually men are hired who can repair as well as operate the somewhat complicated Linotype; typists usually are paid much less than such men.

Larger weeklies soon shifted to offset, and within a few years small daily papers joined the move. Dailies in Dubuque, Iowa, and Oklahoma City, Oklahoma, extended offset into the medium-sized field, and the *Sacramento Union*, with about 100,000 circulation, shifted to offset in 1968. One of the giants, the *St. Louis Post-Dispatch*, has started an experiment with offset with special sections. There are now about 400 offset dailies, and a Scripps League executive has predicted that three out of four will go offset before long.

While it is possible that offset will hit the big city, multi-edition newspapers, most of them have decided to stick with letterpress at present; but they remain watchful for labor-saving devices and have adopted many of them.

Big papers continued to use letterpress for several reasons:

1. Until recently, offset presses ran much slower than letterpress, and they are still a little slower.
2. A multi-million dollar investment already has been made in letterpress.
3. The work force is familiar with letterpress operations; retraining would be costly.
4. Type slugs, in contrast to repros, can be treated roughly and used over and over. This is a real aid in changing from edition to edition.
5. Because the actual type is never used on a rotary press, changes in that type can be made while the presses are running.
6. Paper waste is high with offset. Unless pressmen keep a constant ratio between water and ink, sheets come out poorly printed. In letterpress, only ink must be regulated.

Some letterpress operations, nevertheless, use a great deal of cold type. For example, entire ads can be made up with it. The material is photographed and a conventional newspaper engraving is made.

The making of halftones in the offset process is simple. The halftone negative is made as for a photoengraving. Instead of being acid-etched on a plate, the negative is merely pasted into the space left in the full page negative and burned in. When printed the picture appears to be made by a zinc engraving, except that it usually is clearer and sharper. The excellent reproduction of pictures, with 110 to 120 rows of fine dots per inch, is one of the main points in favor of offset (as offset paper can take fine screens). This process also offers benefits with color.

The other advantages of offset are less expensive equipment and usually lower production costs, machinery that is easy to repair, relatively light presses, and flexibility in the use of type.

According to a survey of forty-six editors by the Associated Press Managing Editors Association, editors prefer offset to letterpress once they have changed over. They found the shift less painful than anticipated. A summary of this survey, by D. W. Bowler, editor of the *Billings* (Mont.) *Gazette*, observed that editors have to learn to think offset, and photographers have to learn how to put in the screen as they print pictures. But editors found that it was easier to get fresher news into their pages fast with offset, and they felt that they controlled the offset paper themselves, rather than being at the whim of printers.

Gravure

A third process which has some use on newspapers is *gravure*—also called *intaglio*, from the Italian for "carved in." If recesses are cut into a copper plate and filled with ink, the ink will come off on paper pressed against it. So tiny grooves of different size and depth can be cut by acid to carry different loads of ink. Very fine shading is possible in such printing. *Rotogravure*—sometimes called just *roto*—is a fast rotary-press process popular with magazines and Sunday papers. Fine quality and a variety of colors are possible with roto. Mechanical pasteups are required, so editorial preparation is practically the same for gravure and offset.

Printing measurements

Some printers will say, "Printing is just arithmetic." To some extent this is true. Printers have to measure everything and must calculate how to make the type fit allotted spaces. To give proper instructions to them, the copyeditor needs to know their measuring system.

The two main printing dimensions are *points* and *picas*. In general, a point refers to vertical measure. One point equals one-seventy-second of an inch. Seventy-two-point type, then, is one inch high. Thirty-six-point is half an inch. Twenty-four-point is one-third of an inch. Most *body type*—the type of news stories—is 8- to 10-point.

The measure for horizontal distance is *pica*. A pica is one-sixth of an inch, so a column two inches wide will have type set 12 picas wide. A half-column cut in such a column width would be 6 picas, or one inch.

A few simple problems and answers will help make these measurements clear.

1. If body type is 9-point, how many lines will there be in three column inches?
2. If a cut is three inches wide, how many picas is it?
3. If the body type of a story is nine inches long and the story has a three-line 36-point type headline, what is the total length of story and headline in inches?
4. How many inches of type will eighteen lines of 8-point make?

The answers: 1. 24; 2. 18; 3. 10-1/2; 4. 2.*

---

* 1. Three times 72 points gives 216 points for three inches. Divide that by nine to get the number of lines. 2. Since an inch is 6 picas, three times six is the number of picas in three inches. Three lines of 36-point would be 108 points. Seventy-two goes into that one-and-a-half times. So add one-and-a-half inches to nine to get the total. 4. Eight times 18 points gives 144 points. Divide by seventy-two to convert to inches.

A pica sometimes is called an *em*. An em technically is the square of the type. Thus, an em of 18-point type is 18 points square—18 points by 18 points. An em of 12-point is 12 points square. A 12-point em, of course, is also a pica wide, because it is one-sixth of an inch. (The em got its name from the letter M, which usually looks as wide as it is high.)

Careful measurement is necessary because most newspapers fit copy to the available space. For example, if a ten-inch hole exists, an editor will send the composing room a story to fit that space. He can determine the length of the story by counting the number of type-written lines; or perhaps he has devised a special ruler to measure copy. Four lines of copy often will equal one inch of type. This kind of measure is inexact, so the story may be a few lines too long or a few lines too short. If it is too long, a makeup man will have to remove a sentence or two. If too short, the story can be *leaded* (pronounced "ledded"). This means that thin pieces of type metal, 1 or 2 points in thickness, are inserted between paragraphs to expand it ("lead it out"). If the story has nine paragraphs and 2-point leads are used, the leading will add 16 points to the story, or about two lines in all. This may not be enough to make the type snug in the forms. So leads may be placed to separate the lines of the first paragraph, the lines of the headline, and the space between the head and the story.

The well-edited paper does not use so much lead that white spaces fragment the stories. Neither does it stick meaningless little fillers into the bottom of the page to report, say, on the number of miles of paved road in Sumatra. A good staff can produce quality "shorts" which use space better than remote facts or mere lead.

Leading, of course, is part of the letterpress process. Offset uses a similar technique. Instead of creating space with lead, the person pasting up the dummy will snip a story into paragraphs and paste each paragraph a tiny distance from the one adjoining. The little extra space adds up to the equal of a few lines.

Types of type

Quality newspapers usually spend much effort on the appearance of their pages. Part of this job is the selection of type. At the turn of the century body type was small and crowded. Headline faces were squeezed thin, and there was so much of this type that the reader could hardly make out what was printed. Gradually the 7-point body type was replaced by 7-1/2- or 8-point type, and that frequently gave way to 9. Today many papers use 9-1/2- or 10-point; or they may use 9-point on a 10-point slug—meaning that the type is 9-point with a point of leading. According to the Research Institute of the American Newspaper Publishers Association, the median type size used by U.S. and Canadian papers rose from 7-1/2 point in 1950 to 8-1/2 point fifteen years later, with two out of five papers using 9-point. Most editors in the seventies will probably be working with type of 9-point or larger.

Similarly, the old all-capital headlines, with layers of decks have given way to simple, neatly designed type faces and headline forms

1. 𝔗𝔢𝔵𝔱

2. Roman

2a. Oldstyle
2b. Modern
2c. Mixed
2d. Italic

3. Gothic

3a. Sans Serif
3b. Sq. Serif

4. Script, Cursives

5. 𝕹𝕺𝖁𝕰𝕷𝕿𝖄

that can be read at a glance. The result has been newspaper pages with white space for "air," body type that can be read without squinting, and heads that have clean beauty. (See figs. 9-8 and 9-9.)

Fig. 4-8. Races of type (left). Five major subdivisions, or "races," of type are illustrated. Square serif type, here a subcategory (3b), is sometimes called a race. The fifth race, novelty, sometimes goes by "ornamented" or other names. Most newspaper usage is obviously in categories 2 and 3—roman and gothic. In common back-shop parlance "italic" is not a subdivision of roman, as shown, but a slanted, or non-perpendicular, form of roman or gothic faces.

U.S. Plan May Start Viet Talks

Tempo bold condensed

Onassis Airliner Hijacked

Vogue

A New Moon View

Century

TRAFFIC DEATH TOLL IS AT 155

Gothic

U.N. Hears Israel Protest Arab Tactics

Bodoni face is used by dozens of American newspapers.

KENNEDY GAINING SUPPORT IN FIGHT TO DEPOSE LONG

Latin style

Texas Asks $10 Billion Water Plan

Cheltenham

Antismoking Campaigners See Progress

Century condensed

Fig. 4-9. Headline faces. Races of type (see fig. 9-8) are divided into families. Loosely called simply "faces," they often bear the name of the designer. This illustration shows some of the common headline faces in use. Note that some have serifs and some do not—that, therefore, they are roman or sans serif.

Many papers, however, have a long way to go, and more research on both the readability of type and the techniques of makeup will stimulate further changes. The current shift by many papers from the 11- or 12-pica column to the 16-pica width is one example of typographic change. Another is the *W-format*—six columns set normal width and the seventh set wider. Still another is the *seven format*, which gives seven columns the space normally given to eight. The extra space makes white "rules" between columns.

Headline faces as big as 36-point can be produced for letterpress on a Linotype and for offset on a machine that turns out cold type heads on a strip of film. Both of these methods are fast and flexible. When the page plates have been made, the type for letterpress can be melted for re-use. (The film for offset is thrown away.) For their biggest heads most letterpress papers handset some pre-cast type called *foundry type*, or even wooden type. The printer picks up each letter and puts it in the page form. After the page is stereotyped, he returns each to its bin in the type case. This is a slow process, too expensive to use more than once or twice a day.

Other large headlines and much advertising type are set on a machine called a *Ludlow*. (See fig. 9-10.) A printer picks matrices, similar to Linotype mats, from a case and puts them in a row, then uses the machine to squeeze molten metal against them to produce slugs several inches long. The mats can be redistributed to the case immediately. The slugs are much easier to handle than foundry type because they are big. (When hand-set type such as foundry spills, the resulting mess is *pied* type—past tense of pi.) Ludlow slugs save time and effort another way because they can be melted down once the page is stereotyped, which frees the printer from having to redistribute the type by hand.

Fig. 4-10. Ludlow. From the trays of type (right) the Ludlow operator gets mats which he places in a stick, which the machine (left) casts into slugs of type.

A machine called an *Elrod* is common in letterpress, though it never actually prints anything. The Elrod creates column rules, simple ad borders, leads to separate type, and base material used to raise engravings and castings type high. It is automatic, needing a printer only to change the dies that turn out the various kinds of metal strips and to remove the finished products from the machine.

Format

In a William Allen White memorial lecture at the University of Kansas, Gardner Cowles, president of the *Des Moines Register* and *Tribune* and editorial chairman of *Look*, commented:

> Newspaper pages today—with few exceptions—are made up, or "designed," by an old-time journeyman-printer and a make-up editor who may, or may not, know much about typography and the thousand and one methods for making pages look readable and exciting. On successful magazines, the art director ranks right below the top editor in importance and authority. He has a strong voice in helping decide how a story idea is to be developed. He suggests ways to give it maximum visual impact. He knows how to blend type and photographs so each helps the other. His responsibility is to make each page come alive and intrigue the reader. Newspapers need this kind of talent. Too few have it.

Whether or not it has a regular art director, a newspaper should certainly have expert advice if it plans to change format. The editors then will chip in with their advice, and its usefulness will depend on how much they have kept up on the printing arts. The better papers are ever alert to the possibility of improvement by typographic change. As noted already, the *Louisville Courier-Journal* went to six-column format in 1965. *Newsday*, a Long Island, New York, tabloid, shifted to magazine-style front page and inside makeup in 1968. In 1969 the *Chicago American* changed from full-size to tabloid, taking the name *Chicago Today*, in an effort to keep alive in a city down to four major dailies.

Color

The comic pages of newspapers pioneered color reproduction, but magazines, using higher quality paper, long ago passed the dailies in use of color, and more recently color television has contributed to making the newspaper's gray image look very old-fashioned. The newspaper magazine of the trade, *Editor & Publisher*, has warned against this color competition and in 1955 began an annual special issue on color to promote its use in dailies.

ROP (run-of-the-paper) color is that printed on the paper's regular newsprint, in ads or editorial. SpectaColor and Hi-Fi are trade names for preprinted color, which can be on higher quality paper. "Preprint" refers to the use of a paper roll already carrying full-color printing by roto, or sometimes by offset, which is fed into the presses and folded into the paper along with regular newsprint.

Editor & Publisher says that nine out of ten dailies now offer ROP color. More than half of these provide for *process color*, which uses three colors in addition to black. The eye blends dots of the three primary colors as well as of black to make the different hues and shades of a conventional colored photograph or painting. More papers provide black plus only one or two colors, for *flat color*, also called *spot color*. Red alone, for example, will make a vivid headline or rule. Two ads using flat color won *Editor & Publisher* color contests. One featured a shirt printed flat blue and the other a sporting figure in rose-red behind a black-and-white car.

Color printing requires a separate press plate for every basic color: red, yellow, and blue—with black the fourth color. Other colors are made by overlapping the basic colors. When two color plates are to print overlapping impressions, great care must be taken to get the plates in *register*. This means, for example, that the blue and yellow impressions must coincide exactly to produce a green. Otherwise the printed picture will appear fuzzy. For example, a register only slightly off on the picture of a woman's green dress can give the garment two distinct hemlines, one yellow and one blue.

Register is so difficult that once a color picture or ad is adjusted properly no editor should tinker with it. If, for example, a color picture is running in columns one through four on page one in the first edition, it had better stay there in later editions—unless an editor is willing to argue with an outraged pressman, who probably has a large metal tool in his hand.

Advertising lineage in ROP color has gone up sharply. It increased steadily more than six-fold for fifteen years after 1951, until a slight temporary dip occurred in 1967, according to annual surveys by *Editor & Publisher*. The increasing use of color by newspaper advertisers means that editors can add color more easily to news pages. A press prepared to print colored ads is prepared to print other items in color.

It is perhaps surprising that some of the biggest papers in the nation are not the biggest users of color. Neither the *Wall Street Journal* nor the *New York Times* is equipped to use color in regular news pages. The *Daily News* and the *Post* in New York were late in providing even spot color. But the *Miami Herald* and *Nashville Tennesseean*, as well as the *Milwaukee Journal* and *St. Petersburg Times*, each report use of up to two thousand color pictures a year.

The Associated Press and United Press International distribute duplicate color transparencies on many subjects, but their executives complain that many clients do not use them. In one period the UPI experimented by moving a color photo daily but use was disappointing. This service sent out an exclusive picture of a woman leaping from a brightly burning building. Though more than a thousand papers got it, only one tear sheet, indicating use, came in. UPI, nevertheless, sends three or four color pictures in a typical week.

"It seems," said Charles J. McCarty, assistant general manager of UPI Newspictures, "that every newspaper editor talks about wanting more editorial color illustration but few of them actually use it. We transmit more color now than ever before, but the percentage of use remains the same or less." In 1967 a *Chicago Tribune* executive, complaining that color was still "the exception, not the rule," said that newspapers were still essentially black-and-white products which compared badly with the wealth of color in magazines.

One problem with color is that it takes time. A picture agency must break a color photograph down into its basic colors, so the newspapers can use a different ink with each of them. It formerly took UPI two hours to make such color separations and a black-and-white photo print of each, but the service then developed a Polaroid method which cut the time below thirty minutes. Then recently UPI started sending three color separations on one picture, in twelve minutes, twenty-four minutes less than when three pictures had been sent. Electronic scanners that make plates even as separations are made offer exciting possibilities. The *Sunday News-Journal* of Daytona Beach, Florida, boasted in 1968 that on two successive weekends it ran color photos of sporting events within five hours of the events' starting times. In short, as time problems are solved, editors may use color more freely.

Quality is another problem. Since ordinary newsprint requires a coarse screen, the illusion of solid color is hard to create. Register also may be poor. Indeed, one of the advantages of offset is that it can use finer screens for better color as well as clear photos. After lengthy experimentation with its letterpress color, the *Philadelphia Bulletin*, having won eleven first prizes with its color, claims it has received twice as many ROP color awards as any other American paper—and its color is good. One of its women's pages, for example, features attractive girls garbed in bright red, yellow, and green against a background of natural-looking bricks and furniture. Though the *Bulletin's* ROP uses ordinary newsprint, the flesh tones are truer than those on most color TV sets.

The New York Press Association has taken special note of two small offset dailies with good four-color reproduction of pictures—the *Tonawanda News* (circulation 18,400) and the *Ithaca Journal* (17,200). The *Monterey* (Calif.) *Peninsula-Herald* (28,600) also does a superb job with color.

SpectaColor art—preprinted by either roto or offset on fine paper—is usually thought of for advertising, but it has been used for editorial. The difficulty is that such illustrations have to be planned well ahead. The *Detroit Free Press* introduced editorial SpectaColor in the spring of 1965 with a six-column, front-page picture of a pretty girl and flowers, and since then has regularly planned such art three to six weeks ahead for many events. The enthusiastic response of readers to this high-quality color is typified by the comment by one letter-writer on that first picture: "It is pure sunshine and spring!"

The editor of tomorrow, more than his predecessor, will use pictures and color to make his pages compete more effectively with magazines and TV.

What of tomorrow?

Despite the introduction of color, TTS, cold type, and offset, newspapers still operate pretty traditionally. Vermont Royster, editor of the *Wall Street Journal*, wrote not long ago: "The newspaper industry is about the only one in America that made no important technological progress from about 1880, the date of Mergenthaler's handy-dandy gadget, until the day before yesterday."

Can the newspaper catch up? Royster indicated there would be glorious days ahead if editors learned to use the new tools.

Some prophets foresee the end of the newspaper as it is now known. They expect to see the disappearance of the whole composing and press room sections as newspapers dispense with typesetting and presses. Instead, they believe that each home or business might have its own little news box, out of which would come a paper stream of printed news, editorials, feature stories, pictures, and advertisements. This strip would be perforated about every twelve inches so it could be torn into segments and bound to resemble a modern magazine. Operating all day long, and most of the night, the machine could handle both bulletin news and detailed news analyses. This instrument could provide all the speed of radio-television news plus the benefits of depth reporting that the better papers now provide. Like the newspaper, it would also be a semi-permanent record; any reader could refer to it a week later or ten years later.

Fig. 4-11. Facsimile. The Asahi Shimbun of Tokyo recently demonstrated a facsimile receiving set for the home. Like radio and TV, it offers the news rapidly and directly. It has the added feature of giving the subscriber "hard copy" that he can mark, cut, save, or recopy.

This device is no dream. It has been possible since 1940, but no one has had both the nerve and the capital to try it commercially. The system, called *facsimile*, transmits the "newspaper" either by wire or radio. Japanese newspapers are now developing facsimile

Facsimile

transmission to homes (fig. 9-11) after having used it to transmit a facsimile, or picture, of each page to a remote printing plant, where plates made from the pictures print the actual newspaper. The *Wall Street Journal* does the same thing by transmitting pictures of some of its editions to other printing plants.

Will facsimile ever replace the conventional newspaper thrown upon millions of porches morning and night? Some think that if facsimile ever comes it will start with the business community. After all, financial needs stimulated the development of telegraphic news services and, indeed, of the newspaper itself. Many offices already have teleprinters bringing them news of the stock market and general business. Dow-Jones, owner of the *Wall Street Journal*, provides this service. But what if Dow-Jones decided to replace the noisy teleprinters, which spew out unattractive type copy, with facsimile? Instead of rolls of wire copy, there could be neat sheets of attractively printed material, including pictures, graphs, and illustrated economic analyses.

If facsimile were accepted in the business community, perhaps some daring newspaper owner would adopt it. Every subscriber, given a little box for receiving the news, would pay a monthly bill for service, like a telephone bill. When his box ran out of paper, he could buy a fresh supply at the supermarket. The great capital outlay of starting such a system is, of course, the major factor blocking it. However, problems of delivery trucks in traffic and getting distributors are a powerful push against this block.

Cable television

The other main possibility for a shift from the traditional newspaper is cable television. When many communities complained about poor television reception, someone hit on the idea of putting up a high tower to receive signals well and then connecting the tower to individual sets by wire. Some of these cable TV firms have permission from the Federal Communications Commission to make special broadcasts, such as high school football games or a hot city council meeting. These same cable TV companies sometimes show news direct from the AP or UPI wires. The TV cameras focus on the copy, and the viewer simply reads the wire report from the screen.

This is already a crude sort of "electronic newspaper," of course, but there is no technical reason why it could not become sophisticated. The wire copy could be typed in a neat, appealing form. Pictures could be interspersed with the text. Editorials, advertising, and comics could appear on the screen. This kind of transmission would require that the subscriber be present to "read" the news. But there is no reason why a paper print could not be made of the newscast by having some attachment on the television set. Or the telecast could be taped and the individual could run the tape through an attachment on his own set whenever he wanted to review the news.

Both facsimile and cable-television newspapers are being considered with some earnestness by big city papers, particularly afternoon papers, which have so much trouble distributing a half million papers through crowded city streets. In New York, for example, it is an ordeal to deliver afternoon papers. Some of the big papers near New York, such as the *Newark News*, have the same trouble. Chicago is not much better. Field Enterprises, which owns the *Chicago Daily News* and the *Chicago Sun-Times*, was so fearful of having the afternoon *Daily News* choked by traffic problems that it set up two suburban dailies in 1966 and another in 1968. The idea was to have a toehold in the suburbs in case the *News* circulation continued to skid. Fortunately for them, the circulation steadied, or another center city daily might have died.

It seems likely that if facsimile or cable-TV "newspapers" develop as general circulation enterprises, they will start in the metropolitan centers. These areas have the potential for subscribers and for investment capital. The start will probably be a small scale experiment launched by an established firm, one with money to risk and with bold executives who can be freed to spend months and even years on development.

Satellite printing plants, pioneered by the big Japanese dailies, may soon solve some problems. The satellite plant can, in some cases, help distribution. The *Los Angeles Times* operates a satellite plant, without using facsimile, in Orange County, south of the city. While this has been working well for the *Times*, it requires an astounding investment in presses and other equipment plus, of course, labor. Satellite plants were considered for the Chicago suburbs by Field but rejected as impractical; the suburbs covered too big an area.

These changes are often considered because they are immediately possible—or nearly so. But some entirely new process may be just over the horizon. The big electronic companies are working in tandem with some of the big publishing houses in an attempt to produce startling changes in printing. They may come up with devices that will truly revolutionize the newspaper business. The inventions may be so innovative, and the output of the new equipment so inexpensive, that the change will sweep the country, as television did in the late 1940s.

The journalism student of today is bound to be plunged into changes. This does not mean that he will have to learn the complexities of new equipment any more than an automobile driver has to know how his newest car operates. The typical journalist, like the typical car driver, needs a basic knowledge of what the machines can do. And he must consider not only how they can work for him, but how they can work in the best interests of the public.

The basics of graphic arts will be important to any conceivable graphic presentation of the future. We have known students who saw no practical use for learning about type and layout, but on the job the background has proved useful in unexpected ways—like making up printed blurbs for TV commercials! Without such knowledge and a continuing interest in the effects of technical change, a copyeditor will fall behind in the task of efficiently bringing the news to his community.

5 The editor and journalistic writing

Editors on newspapers deal with writers and their writing in a number of ways, the most obvious being copyediting. The first three chapters covered problems of correcting and improving news stories; now we focus on more theoretical or philosophical problems. Copyeditors and other influential editorial employees must develop a philosophy of newswriting style, inculcate their ideas in their writers, and guide them toward the production of better writing.

The relationship of editor and writer may be on a one-to-one basis. Traditionally, the city editor assigns a reporter to a story and then sees that he does the job well. But as newspaper journalism becomes more and more thorough, an editor plays the role of a good athletic coach or committee chairman. A sub-editor, perhaps in consultation with the managing editor, decides whether to put two or three reporters on a series covering an important subject, or to organize a team for a complete investigation. Then he provides the leadership for the creation of the copy until it is finally edited and published.

Team leadership

As discussed in chapter 14, an editor should recognize and develop good ideas for major stories. Sometimes a subject is a natural because an alert reporter brings in a tip from some contact, and the appropriate editor simply has to give him the green light for time to dig into the question. The assistant city editor may hatch the idea for a great series while he is driving to work. Some of the best ideas may develop as a few editors and reporters are lunching, or perhaps talking shop at a picnic.

But as newspapers move to develop more and better interpretive and specialized pieces, editors have to set aside time to be creative and work out ideas. The newspaper office has traditionally been too hectic for other than the obvious ideas to be recognized. While some newspapers show initiative, in the last decade or two it often has been the magazine editor or the producer of an occasional TV documentary who has launched the really penetrating studies on subjects like violence or poverty. To be similarly effective, the newspaper editor must seek the quiet to ruminate about his community and trends and the problems of his neighbors and himself, and so discover what his readers need to know more about. The idea for an investigation of teen-age use of a new drug will probably hit any editor in the eye. But some knowledge of social developments and some pondering probably are necessary to recognize the need for a series on abortions among the community's women, changing rates of illegitimacy, or the fate of adoptable babies.

Perspective reporting

It can be argued that interpretive reporting is just good reporting. It is true that "in-depth" or "enterprise reporting" or "backgrounder" may simply be a fancy title for the old-fashioned digging which was a part of any good newswriting any time. Yet the complexity of modern issues and the social need to understand them require more resources, more reporters, more thought, and more leadership. Wes Gallagher, general manager of the Associated Press, has pointed to the shift toward investigative reporting and what he calls "perspective reporting."

"Today's problems are much more complex and investigation of them takes a lot more time and effort," he said in a William Allen White Memorial Lecture. "It is a rare case when one reporter can gather enough facts in a short time and come up with a story that will be authentic enough to convince and hold the attention of our new readers. . . . We can convince only by the most detailed presentation of facts, for facts alone have the ring of truth." It took months, he said, for the AP to develop a story of graft in Vietnam which ran on most of the front pages of the U. S. While the main job was done by two men, many others had a part. He continued:

> The other great weapon that we have is perspective reporting that can and must be used on the daily flow of news. . . . Perspective reporting is presenting news in its proper relationship to the whole and in relation to other news in its own time. Perspective reporting dissects the situation today and compares it with the past. . . . Perspective reporting requires a cold, logical approach to the news. It requires dogged pursuit of facts until the writer is convinced that he has everything he can possibly dig out. The facts must then be sorted and logically presented.

A sample investigation

Gallagher complained, for example, that the federal government was simply too big to be covered. There were 1,222,000 employees in the Department of Defense, he said, 80,000 in Agriculture, and so on. To deal with that coverage problem, the AP established a Washington-based group of ten top reporters, called the Special Assignment Team. Its head, Ray Stephens, a man in his forties with about two decades of AP experience, says its job is to ignore deadlines and look for "the submerged dimension" of the federal government. Its stories have made nation-wide headlines, such as "U.S. Military Fuel Stolen in Thailand" and "Study Shows Waste by Pentagon." Team members get leads to such stories by reading government reports or sometimes by tips from highly-placed friends. Then, like police investigators, team members conduct lengthy interviews and check published materials. In one instance, two members spent five months digging, which included line-by-line reading of fifteen volumes of hearing transcripts.

Under the direction of the metropolitan editor, four writers for the *New York Times* produced a 30,000-word report for the paper on a scandal in the city's Human Resources Administration. Some three months of work began on an October 18 when Metropolitan Editor Art Gelb wrote a memo telling Richard Reeves, city hall bureau chief, to take a look. A tip from Reeves and a word dropped from a city official to a magazine writer persuaded him that the anti-poverty program was in a "ghastly mess." Later, Gelb added Barnard L. Collier to the job. By mid-December there was considerable material, and Gelb deployed Richard Phalon from the city financial beat and Richard Severo of criminal court beat to join the team.

In early January Gelb told the foursome to get out of the office and not come back until ready to write. Five days later, after midnight, the four phoned Gelb from a Chinese restaurant in New Jersey that they were ready and had to see him right away.

> "Right away" turned out to be dinner that night at the Gelbs' apartment when Barbara [Gelb] joined a support team that finally included Beverly Collier and Carol Reeves—whose homes were invaded by the strangest men—Barbara Campbell, who shifted our phone calls from the office to a dozen weird places and then held us together for the first week of writing, Linda Lake, our blushing researcher who learned words they don't teach in Library Science, George Barrett, who read and reread every one of our 30,000 words, John Darnton and Jim Sterba, who did some fine reporting, Marty Tolchin, who faithfully recorded every nasty thing the mayor and Mitch Ginsberg (HRA administrator) said about us, and Steve Roberts, who was followed by Los Angles police as he tracked down a West Coast lead. The L. A. cops faithfully reported to New York authorities that Steve was staying at a "motel" with a woman "unknown locally." It was his wife, Cokie.
>
> There were also honorary team members in the highest and lowest places who might be embarrassed, fired, or indicted if we revealed what they told us or did for us.

Gelb moved the team into a conference room next to the sports department and set the clock half an hour ahead each afternoon to get copy moving earlier. He talked the other editors into allotting more or less unlimited space. It appeared that part of the scandal involved a plot to embezzle a million dollars and transfer it from city accounts to a bank in Zurich, so the *Times* pulled its foreign desk into the story. "There was something satisfying about working on an investigation and having some of the best professionals in the law enforcement business calling you for information. And that's the way it was on the Swiss bank caper." (The team won the 1968 Byline Award of the New York Newspaper Reporters Association.)

Investigative leadership

The editor's role in such investigative or interpretive reporting is that of any good team leader. He goads, he persuades, he inspires, he pushes. He supervises the collection of data, on the theory that two or more editoral heads are better than a single reporter's. He works over drafts to see that there are no holes—and no libel. He asks the questions that even the best team of investigators may not think of. The editor puts together his own experience in reporting and editing and his knowledge of the community to make sure the staff has done its best.

Sometimes the editor must use a firm hand to get the production the community deserves. In one middle-sized city the social welfare reporter got the go-ahead to do a series on Negro employment in local business and industry. He was so thorough that he conducted scores of interviews over several weeks. As time passed, the information in the early interviews began to get stale. The paper's interest flagged, perhaps in part because the lengthy investigation brought worried inquiries from industrial leaders. When the brief series finally appeared, it was weak—much weaker than if done with more dispatch. Perhaps the city editor should have assigned a second reporter to help collect information. Perhaps the editor should have told the reporter at a certain point, "You've got enough material. Write it!" In any event, firm and courageous editorial leadership was missing.

Aides of the team

Editors also have leadership roles with various non-staffers. As indicated in chapter 8, the state editor may have to teach the country correspondent the basics of straight writing. Steady, clear communication is essential to lead a team of part-time stringers. Similarly, a good foreign desk provides leadership for its foreign correspondents —staff and stringer. One of the major complaints of reporters who write abroad is that the home office does not communicate but leaves them too much on their own.

Free-lance writers and photographers also can be valuable. They should be treated courteously even if the paper can use only a little free-lance work, and they should be encouraged and guided if the quality of work is poor but promising.

Amateurs should be given pointers about producing the articles or pictures the paper can use. The roto magazine of the *Houston Chronicle* has a form that explains its needs in subjects, pictures, manuscript preparation, and deadlines, and its method of payment. Queries on ideas should be answered, not ignored. Rejected material should be sent back promptly, even if the editor is busy and overburdened, and checks ought to be mailed quickly for accepted material. The smart editor supplements his regular staff operation when he provides effective leadership for the part-timers and free-lances.

The editor as teacher

More advanced editors in various slots must serve as instructors in English and journalism, especially with greener reporters. At worst this teaching is hit or miss; at best it must be sandwiched into the few moments that editors and writers can find together in their busy schedules.

The editor first of all has to be clear what his goals are for good writing. Does he want thoroughness, brightness, or both? Then, in countless observations, corrections, criticisms, and sermonettes, he shows his writers how they are, and are not, measuring up.

Outlines and structures

Every journalistic neophyte soon learns, if he does not already know, that news stories are constructed on the pattern of the "inverted pyramid." The most important facts go into the first paragraph, or lead, and other information follows in short paragraphs of less and less importance so the pattern can be diagrammed as a triangle standing on its point, a two-dimensional inverted pyramid. The perceptive editor discovers soon enough, if he has not already learned it as a reporter, that this pattern applies only to the simplest news items, unless "inverted pyramid" is understood in the most general terms, as different stories require different forms.

Traditionally, the feature story has always been an exception. The writer can start a feature with a question or an anecdote or a quote, among other devices, and he may write chronologically or according to some other non-triangular logic. Sometimes features are diagrammed as pyramids sitting on their bases, but this schematization is no more applicable universally than the triangle is to news stories. An editor who started to revise a feature to fit any such preconceived pattern would soon stop, frustrated and foolish.

What, then, *can* an editor discover about the structure of complicated stories, and what can he hope to teach his advanced reporters?

In his popular English textbook, *The Practical Stylist*, Prof. Sheridan Baker of the University of Michigan argues that the writer should find a *thesis* to begin his piece. A thesis can be stated as a debate resolution, "Resolved that . . ." When the writer thus clarifies his aim, he finds that the supportive information falls into logical order, into an outline.

This approach has some validity for most news stories, since the beginning states the point of each piece (though not argumentatively as the word *thesis* implies). The concept is most applicable to the work of the editorial writers when they attempt persuasive editorials, but in the newsroom Baker's thesis on theses is generally valuable. It reminds editors to look for clear exposition of the main point close to the top of a story.

Another rhetorical tradition classifies writing forms, such as the essay, into a natural (and obvious) pattern of three parts—beginning, middle, and end, standing like three rectangular blocks piled one on another. The middle block might be subdivided into several flat rectangles (or paragraphs) of development. The bottom block is conclusion. This plan fits nicely with Baker's, if the top block contains the statement of thesis.

This tripartite form again may seem more suited to essays for the editorial page than for front-page news accounts. The shift toward more and more interpretation, however, makes this observation less and less certain. What is a series of articles but a number of blocks? And as background, depth, and perspective become the writer's watchwords, he is less concerned with the first-paragraph punch of the inverted-pyramid and more concerned with the clarity emphasized in the beginning-middle-end structure.

Complex patterns

Analysis of news stories over many decades shows that actually they are not simple triangles. Usually they are a number of triangles on a string, like fish. The story unfolds in two or three paragraphs, then recaps with more detail, explains at length in a third triangle, and perhaps adds minor detail and color in still another. Consider the story of a major fire in three or four buildings. The first section quickly recounts the deaths and damage. The next section reveals how it started and spread and how fire-fighting forces were marshalled. The next triangles tell who discovered it, of the efforts to confine it to the first building, and of a call for outside help. There may be a snippet about two suburbs that sent equipment and men. A block of type may inquire into insurance. Then in more leisurely fashion the writer may present the whole chronology again, quoting the passerby who thought he saw smoke, the watchman who opened the inner doors and discovered the blaze, or the woman who threw her baby into the fire net.

The story may form a more complicated pattern than even a series of triangles, as figure 15-1 suggests. A triangle that tapers off to the inconsequential point would bore a reader. Rather, each triangle becomes blunt-bottomed. Some are hardly triangles at all. Can a chronological account be called a triangle, since start, middle and finish are equally essential to the tale? Is a list of injured a triangle? Blocks and wedges are more appropriate to clear portrayal of the way a long story is put together.

The copyeditor who sees news articles in some such schematic fashion will understand better how they can be tightened and rearranged. Perhaps the inner logic requires that a paragraph or two near the end be moved up to a higher position, even though these sentences are in themselves quite trivial. Or perhaps cutting a minor detail in the heart of the story will strengthen the whole.

An editor able to analyze advanced writing can quickly show reporters where their work is solid and where it is loose or rambling. His analytic skill is especially useful in working with an investigative team. Structuring the long series becomes like outlining a lengthy magazine article or the book. Formal logic has to be related to the likelihood that a reader's interest will wane, and to the technical demand that the individual pieces be a certain length. "Can we shift this block into the first article in the series, and can we give the third piece some punch by building up this anecdote?" Sometimes these deceptively simple questions lead his writing team into a type of outline they hoped to have left in Freshman English.

It may be useful to think of the modern news story not as a triangle but as a freight train: The diesel supplies the power and the pace, and a series of boxes follow with the information. More than other types of writing, news stories have minimal transitions and internal references. With little concern, a copyeditor can shift paragraphs around. The building blocks of many stories seem almost interchangeable. To the extent that the news fits this train pattern, writer and editor both can shunt the box cars in and out of the line, pushing those with the less important freight to the end, where an editor or printer can uncouple the last few.

Fig. 5-1.   Story patterns. These patterns are a more realistic picture of complex news stories than the traditional inverted pyramid. The more complex the story, the more likely it is a combination of triangles, wedges, and rectangles. Copyeditors who recognize these variations will be able to reshape a story effectively.

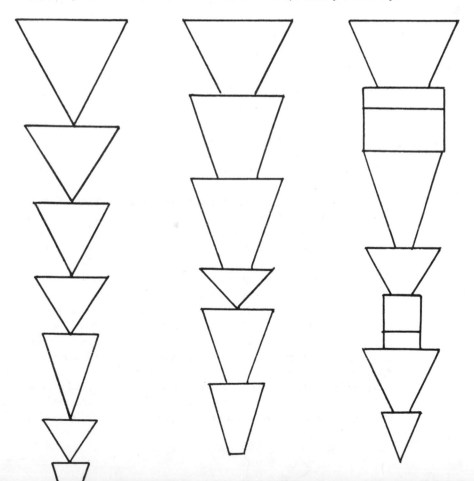

Whatever the pattern, the story must be logical. That logic need not be of the I, II, III type. It can be chronological or it can be psychological, in the sense that the reporter moves the reader from one point of interest to another. The chief sin is rambling. It is "circling and droning, reminiscent of buzzards hovering, swooping over a victim until he drops," in the words of a prominent magazine editor and no mean writer himself, Norman Cousins, of the *Saturday Review*. Good organization of thoughts is the key to good written or oral communication, says Cousins, adding: "The prime element in this process is sequence. Ideas have to be fitted together. The movement of a concept or an image from the mind of the speaker to the mind of the listener is retarded when words become random chunks rather than sequential parts of an ordered whole."

Both reporters and editors rarely think of the most effective ways to structure their accounts. They play by ear and do the job as newsmen have for decades. Therefore, the editor-teacher must jog both writers and copyeditors to strive for patterns that will communicate best in today's paper.

More should be done on newspapers to discover fresh, new ways to present material related to a central story, but more variations could be explored. Instead of one long story, why not five short stories which are sidebars to each other? Why not play three or four related stories, perhaps with a box or editorial to explain their common theme?

Magazine editors appear more ambitious in developing new patterns of presentation. They have tried boldface summaries, like precedes, at the top of articles in trade magazines. They have boldfaced the first paragraph of new sections. Some have tried narrative, near-fiction techniques; others have paired two pieces, one light and illustrated, the other serious and editorial. Newspapermen may find stimulating ideas of writing patterns and related graphic displays in the best-edited magazines.

The meanings of style

"Style" is used by newspaper editors in at least two senses. The uniform system of spelling and capitalization is called style, as we discussed in chapter 2 on copyediting, but the form and presentation of newspaper prose are also style.

Good journalistic style is not florid, not ornate, not rhetorical. The late journalism dean Frank Luther Mott used to say, the best journalism is also good literature, as clearly demonstrated in the reporting of Ben Franklin, Stephen Crane, and Ernest Hemingway. English professors have long contended that good prose is usually plain and straightforward and therefore clear. "The approach to style is by way of plainness, simplicity, orderliness, sincerity," says William Strunk, Jr., and E. B. White's *The Elements of Style*. And so it is to good newspaper style too.

Effective prose communicates ideas and information. It might be argued that some English is used to convey an ambiance or feeling without presenting much fact. But such usage in news reports is rare.

Journalistic style has to be functional. The need to quickly convey ideas from one mind to other minds underlies the need for simple, clear writing.

What language scholars call "standard English" is appropriate to newspapers. Neither the formal English of the academic book nor the "non-standard" or colloquial dialect of folksy talk has much place in newspaper pages. For most purposes, reporters and editors should choose their words from the broad range of language understood by most moderately educated people.

Standard English is threatened on the one side by jargon and gobbledegook. Reporters close to many professions may fall into legalese, academic pudder, or bureaucratic gibberish. On the other side is a threat from what has traditionally been known as slang —faddish talk. Noting the likenesses between the academicians and the hip talkers, the editing authority on the *New York Times*, Theodore Bernstein, has pointed out that both groups substitute their own redundant words for normal English. Both have some intent to be secret and so obscure to those not of the in-group. Newspapers must abjure both kinds of fringe English if they are to communicate across the strata of a diverse readership.

Advocates of plain, simple style sometimes face the objection that this kind of writing is dull and lifeless. It need not be. Concrete nouns and strong verbs close to human experience can make a simple sentence vivid and lively. Yet sometimes even a good writer will fill a story with the stereotyped and obvious until it shrivels and dies.

"Over the years, wire service reporting had gotten flat, had leveled off to an efficient but uninspired pattern," said Roger Tatarian, UPI editor, to explain why UPI was shifting its attitude about news presentation to stress readability. To help make its style more human UPI introduced a category, "Personal Report," to personalize stories traditionally done impersonally. Reporters were instructed to write first-hand pieces and even use "I." In a staff memo Tatarian said: "The use of the *I* can be effective only if it is not overdone, and if it is done logically and naturally. There should be enough of it to give the flavor of a letter to the folks at home, but not so much as to make the writer hog the center of the stage."

Other editors might adopt this view as they try to develop reporting styles which are at once simple, lively, clear, readable, and communicative.

The sources of style

An editor's examination of style comes down to his analysis of the grammatical ingredients of the story. As the physicist probes molecules, atoms, and electrons to try to understand matter, the editor digs into paragraphs, sentences, and words. Admittedly, there is a mystic quality in the overall effect of writing, for the whole somehow turns out to be greater than the sum of the parts. Still, some of the mystery can be penetrated by looking at the individual blocks and the ways they fit one another.

Paragraphs   In most writing the paragraph is an obvious fundamental block. The formal outline of an essay or a book divides into topics, sub-topics, and sub-sub-topics; each sub-sub-topic may be treated as a paragraph. Such a unit will have a topic sentence (actually a sub-sub-topic sentence) supported by five or a dozen or more sentences. With proper transitions, such paragraphs clearly reveal the structure and movement of the work.

Such paragraphs set in column widths, even the new-fashioned six-column pages, might each run four or five or even ten inches. Even set in the wider measure used for editorials, they would look forbidding. So newspapermen, including editorial writers, use shorter paragraphs, often only one or two sentences long.

Copy is not effectively formed into short paragraphs by haphazard chopping, as some reporters and copyreaders apparently suppose. Nor is simply breaking most stories into one-sentence paragraphs enough, as it once was in more sensational papers. The best procedure is to search the "normal" paragraph of the topic-sentence variety for the clusters of ideas within it. Thus a twelve-sentence unit may prove to be made up of four to six smaller pieces. Each piece then may become a newspaper-type paragraph, and each may run one or two, perhaps three, sentences, but rarely more. In type the paragraph will be a horizontal rectangle or a square rather than a formidable, vertical oblong. At the same time, if the writer sees the relation of these shorter paragraphs to the overall pattern, he is able to write in a more logical style.

Sentences   A paragraph should rarely run over fifty words. In typescript, a paragraph of four or five lines is beginning to run too long. If such a paragraph has even two or three sentences, they must obviously be short—perhaps an average of fifteen words, though no such figure should be taken arbitrarily. Length is thus one criterion of the good sentence, and newspaper sentences are usually short compared to those in books or scholarly magazines.

Sentences also should be straight—that is, clear and to the point. "English is going to pot, and one of the reasons it's going to pot is the way it's taught," complained Dr. Don Cameron Allen, professor of English at Johns Hopkins University. "I teach students to write a straight sentence. That's what English is all about. You will find excellent examples of good straight sentences in good American newspapers."

Though grammatically most straight sentences are simple, few compound, and even fewer complex, newsmen might pay more attention to what is known in English classes as the periodic sentence. The elements in American sentences are somewhat loosely tied, but not quite haphazard. By contrast, the periodic sentence builds from beginning to end, so the last element is the climax. That gives writing punch, like this: Mayor Jones paused over the document, frowned, and then, as his face and neck reddened, shouted, "Never!" Of course, putting an idea at the start of a sentence also can have impact: "Cut taxes" was the cry of most of those testifying.

Three common faults of newspaper sentences easily identified by the editor-teacher are the *clogged*, the *overburdened* and the *too-complex*.

The clogged sentence simply packs too much information between the capital letter and the period. Writing dense sentences used to be good style but is now old-fashioned. For example, no desk today should pass a sentence with this beginning:

> Jonathan Doakes, 41, of 6357 Harmondale Drive, a carpenter and part-time plumber, who told reporters he had never been in trouble before, and a companion, who gave his name as Samuel Smithson, 53, of 6359 Harmondale Drive, also a carpenter, were arrested today after what was, according to witnesses, a scuffle over the way another neighbor, Clyde Hendricks, 32, of 6358 Harmondale Drive, should build his fences.

The modern way is to rewrite, "Two carpenters were arrested today after a scuffle over the way another neighbor should build his fences." The specifics can wait.

The overburdened sentence, although like the clogged, is not so much packed with facts as overstuffed with ideas. The writer loads too much freight onto the sentence before he hits the period key.

> Like the legislature's redistricting plan of 1969, the proposed new constitutional amendment now before the Senate Judiciary Committee, and soon to go before the House Rules Committee, not only deals with the congressional district problem but also the issue of one-voter-one-vote, according to regulations set by a previous ruling of the Supreme Court.

Break it up, simplify.

The too-complex sentence resembles both the clogged and the overburdened. Its writer is following the dictum to get away from the simple Dick-saw-Jane sentence. It is good advice, especially for essays and editorials, but the newswriter can overdo by throwing in too many clauses and phrases.

> Since the recent outbreak of warfare and because of popular reaction to the news, especially in view of the fact that it came on the heels of revulsion about the pact of Vienna, the Communists and their satellites, not only in Eastern Europe but in much of Asia, have restricted travel by foreign newsmen who will now have to obtain stories from an official press bureau.

Again, break it up.

Writers of these three faulty types of sentences have in common the laudable attempt to pack a lot of information into a short space.

But an overconcentration of facts or ideas or grammatical style makes a story opaque. The antidote in each case is to lighten the load of each sentence. Even the most intelligent reader needs frequent periods to "catch his breath."

A fruitful suggestion for writing better sentences is summarized in the slogan, "One idea, one sentence." Elements in the preceding stories such as the carpenters' addresses, the old redistricting plan, or that Vienna pact should be cut away from the verbose illustrative sentences above. The main idea of each sentence then will stand out so the reader can grasp it quickly.

Editors of the *New York Times* have pushed the one-idea-to-a-sentence theme for several years. Their second-guessing bulletin, *Winners & Sinners*, has occasionally pointed up the value of the concept with illustrations from the paper. Here, for example, is one sentence which would be easier to follow if divided:

> Black nationalism is the dominant mood of the Negro masses in the United States today, according to James Farmer, who warns white liberals in his book, "Freedom —When?" that there will be no respite from demonstrations and other forms of direct action until full equality is achieved.

Here is another sinner from the *Times:*

> In Montreal, leaders of the American Bar Association killed Wednesday a resolution denouncing a key provision of the civil rights bill aimed at preventing discrimination in the selection of Federal jurors.

Of the second example the *W&S* editor commented: "The facts are all there, but the reader has to go to work on them. He has to take it from the bottom: The bill is against discrimination. Fine. But the resolution denounces this provision. Uh-uh. But wait a minute—the bar leaders have killed the resolution. So it's fine again, eh? In other words, the bar leaders took a stand in favor of preventing discrimination in the selection of Federal juries. Why not say it in some form similar to that?"

Words   The strength of sentences depends ultimately on the choice and arrangement of their words. The good editor becomes expert on these basic blocks. Instead of the vague, the abstract, and the unusual, he seeks words which are *direct, concrete,* and *familiar*— words which build vivid and accurate pictures for most readers.

Some editors prefer words of Anglo-Saxon background to those with Latin roots. Generally, pithy words are from Old English, flowery ones from the Romance languages (i.e., those descended from Latin, the language of the Romans). Actually, a combination of words from both streams often most effectively provides variation and texture. Accuracy and strength, as well as commonness, should guide word choice, and vitality in verbs is especially important.

Forms of "to be" are generally static—as in that clause—so editors prefer verbs which act, which suggest movement. One-syllable words often generate the most power. Reducing the sentence usually adds strength. Pare away weak or unnecessary adjectives and adverbs. (If this paragraph demonstrates its own preachments, it is because of vivid words like *roots, pithy, flowery, works, texture, static, guide,* and *pare.*)

Choice of the right word nowadays is complicated by rapid changes in language. Again, a number of guides are available. Published almost a decade ago, the third edition of *Webster's New International Dictionary* embodies mid-twentieth century language and so is available in most newsrooms today. But the third edition gives few value judgments on words. For a more regular, though more conservative evaluation of words, some editors prefer the second edition, compiled in the thirties. A good guide to modern American usage is the *Dictionary of Contemporary Usage* by Bergen and Cornelia Evans. Also valuable is the revision by Sir Ernest Gowers of the famous *Dictionary of Modern English Usage* of H. W. Fowler, a classic in England. Theodore Bernstein of the *Times,* quoted earlier, has three helpful books, the first based on *Winners & Sinners: Watch Your Language, More Language That Needs Watching,* and more recently, *The Careful Writer: A Modern Guide to English Usage.*

Commenting on the last book, literary critic Granville Hicks said that of the six guidelines Bernstein suggests for judging good usage, he preferred this one: *Observation of what makes for clarity, precision, and logical presentation.* Hicks points out that this rule prohibits some newer usages that obscure rather than clarify. While Hicks admits that the misuse of "like" for "as" will not greatly damage the language, he believes that the growing confusion of "infer" for "imply" does debase our common English coin. Such distinctions may seem picky. But effective writing depends upon careful and correct choices precisely at this level of language.

A final word on jargon

As we said before, jargon confuses more than clarifies. In medicine or law, to be sure, a specialized word may add precision. In education, argues Dr. James S. LeSure of the Connecticut Department of Education, jargon actually can confuse even educators. But teachers use phrases like "peer acceptance" and "group practice" because these seem to give them professional status, even though parents don't know what they are talking about. So Dr. LeSure wrote *Guide to Pedaguese,* "a handbook for puzzled parents" that may also help education writers.*

"When you get your degree you can't wear it around your neck to prove you're educated," urban reformer Saul Alinsky wrote in *Harper's* magazine, "so instead you use a lot of three and four-syllable words. Of course, they aren't any use at all if you really want to

---

*The U. S. Government Printing Office issues an inexpensive booklet with similar aims, *Gobbledygook Has Gotta Go* (1966).

communicate with people. You have to talk straight English, using a small word every time you can instead of a big one." Such advice is good not only for educators and sociologists but for reporters and editors. They communicate best when they use simple words in straight sentences in brief but well-organized paragraphs.

Theories of readability

In a computer age when so much of life is quantified, it is tempting to analyze and measure language in the search for better communication. Can English be approached scientifically? Can the clarity or interest of a piece of writing be weighed or measured? Yes and no. No calipers or scales exist to indicate accurately whether sentences convey their message well. But quantification of newspaper copy may help a writer analyze style.

What can be measured? The stylists and critics we have examined indicate the qualities we might hope to quantify: difficulty of words, complexity and density of sentences, use of clichés or jargon, strength of verbs, and so on. The problem with measurement is that many of these stylistic qualities defy objective judgment.

Readability theorists who search for objective measurements have centered on judging the difficulty of words and sentences, which is certainly a key consideration. This factor is measured in the "fog index" developed by Robert Gunning (explained in *The Technique of Clear Writing*) and in the "Flesch formula" described by Rudolf Flesch (in *The Art of Readable Writing* and other books). After study of these and other practical applications of readability theory, Dr. Jeanne S. Chall of Ohio State University identified four significant reliable measurements: vocabulary load, sentence structure, idea density, and human interest. The first two relate to the Gunning-Flesch work, and the third is associated with clogging and overburdening. We shall look at the fourth below.

The Flesch formula

In the late forties AP hired Flesch to advise on improving writing. So practical journalistic use was made of a "readability formula" he had devised. His scheme rests on two assumptions. First, the number of syllables in samples of 100 words each increases as the writing becomes more difficult. Second, the more short sentences in the samples the easier the reading. Actually, short words in short sentences can be hard going, but since the opposite is more often the case, the assumptions seem justified.

Starting with them, one can randomly choose a few samples from news stories, interpretive stories, or editorials. He counts the syllables and the number of sentences (to find average sentence length) and works out the Flesch score according to the mathematics or charts in Flesch's books. If the sentences average fifteen to eighteen words each and if there are 145 to 155 syllables in each sample, the writing scores as "standard" and is suitable for much newspaper writing. Such sentences are not very long, obviously, and such a vocabulary includes a great many one-syllable words. However, using more long words or making the sentences more complex (and

therefore longer) will almost certainly make the writing more difficult.

Paring sentences to an average of twelve words each and vocabulary to 130 or 140 syllables per hundred words results in what Flesch
rates as "easy." If news stories were written at this level—and few
are—less-educated readers would doubtless grasp them more
readily.

The chart in figure 15-2 gives a quick check of readability, according to the ideas of Flesch and Gunning. If the editor selects a random
sample of 100 words of copy, he can count syllables and number of
sentences and plot the coordinates, perhaps with help of an L-shaped
cardboard. An editor should check several samples before making
any generalizations about the paper, and he should consider
hundreds of samples from different pages over a considerable period
of time before determining the readability of his paper needs his
special attention.

Fig. 5-2. **Readability chart.** Count the syllables in a 100-word sample of news copy
and find that number on the horizontal line. Then count the sentences (to nearest
quarter) in the same sample; find that number on the vertical line. The intersection
of the coordinates (a cardboard cut in the shape of "L," as for picture editing, will
help) identifies the simplicity or difficulty of the sample. The graph shows samples
with the following counts plotted to indicate three major categories: Easy, Standard, and Hard (marked with E, S, and H, respectively).

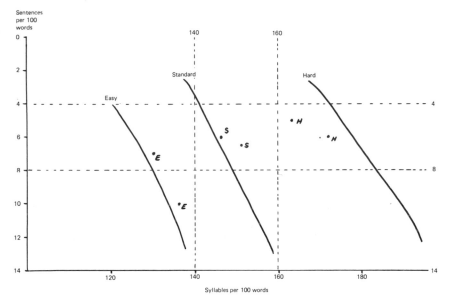

Using the Flesch method, two researchers compared news stories
to editorials in several West Coast dailies. They found both forms
difficult, but the news was actually less readable than the editorials!
"The median readability level of news stories analyzed in this study
indicates that most of them can be readily comprehended by only
those people with a high school diploma or a college education."

Applying the test

Editors want copy which will, as these researchers say, reach "audiences from a wider range than that."

Recognizing that some writing passes muster as "readable" but is still dull, Flesch later developed a "human interest" formula. The most important factor in these measurements are what he calls "personal words"—he, she, Mr. Brown, Susan, etc. He also counts, but gives less weight to, "personal sentences," which include quotations and direct address to the reader. Fortunately, news stories deal with people, so a degree of human interest "comes naturally." However, some writers tend to abstractions, especially in writing of such subjects as government finance or sociology. To counteract this, editors can remind reporters that they must bring human beings into their copy.

Assessing the audience

Being concerned to make news writing easier and more interesting does not mean an editor must seek the lowest common denominator of readership. True, he should provide some material, aside from sports and comics, which is clear even to poorly educated readers. And he should try to reach a broad readership. But some papers that have directed all content toward the "average" person have declined in circulation and general economic health. The successful papers of today continue to improve the quality of content a notch or two every few years. If a newspaper did choose stories for only a ninth grade audience, it would omit much information on science, the arts, serious economics, the inner workings of politics, and dozens of other subjects.

To argue that because the average *formal* educational level of a community is only 10.3 years the paper must be written for high school sophomores assumes that a person learns nothing after he leaves school. It also assumes that those with little schooling and little experience are newspaper readers. It is more realistic to assume that those above average in education and intelligence are the most avid readers. While still including news of interest for those who are not so lucky or concerned, the mix of content should emphasize news for them. Nonetheless, editors should insist that stories always are lively and clear, as well as fact-filled. Even the most intelligent reader, who is able to cope with a scholarly journal, may be pestered with distractions while reading his newspaper. Like everyone else, he must sometimes get the facts from his paper without much concentration. This means that the writing must be appealing and easy.

But Tom Wicker of the *New York Times* is right when he says, "Nobody yet ever made a writer out of a hack by setting up rules. . . . And to the man who tells me that every story can be written in 600 words, or 750, or whatever, I say that that is merely a rule; and I take my stand with Joseph Pulitzer, who said with a writer's exactness and a lawyer's flexibility that the prescription was 'terseness—intelligent, not stupid, condensation.'" Neither readability nor human interest concepts should be viewed as magic cure-alls. They can help newspapermen check on their talent for good copy, and no more. The good editor, as captain of his team, must above all continue to study overall story organization and the effective use of style.

Appendix a: tips for copyeditors

Most editors-in-chief tell their copyeditors to "use words correctly." Good advice, of course, but hard to follow. What is correct? Who said so? What about new words not yet in dictionaries? Which dictionary is correct? Not only are there new words, but new meanings of old words, as with *hip, cool,* and *pot.*

Newspapers use a standard for the meanings of words. If they did not, the reader would be confused frequently by jargon, slang, and malapropism. Usually the standard is the big dictionary in the middle of the newsroom, even if the edition is twenty years old. Some supplement is needed, however, to cover words newly accepted into the written language. On the other hand, an editor should take care to avoid words or meanings that he thinks will appear for a short time and then pass into obscurity even as they are being listed in a new dictionary. Perhaps a good guide to word usage in a newspaper would be to cling to the old, so the meaning of language does not change every generation, but adapt to the new if it brings freshness and vividness to the language.

Editors should not only be alert to changing usage, they should spot redundancies, grammatical errors, and misleading language. To this end we offer the following tips on usage, grammar, and spelling.

The following words and phrases are often mistakenly used.   Usage

Actual fact or *true fact.* A fact is by definition true.
Advise, for *inform.* "He was *informed* [not *advised*] of his wife's illness
    and *advised* to call her doctor immediately."
Alternative, for *alternate.* "He had an *alternate* [not *alternative*] plan.
    It gave the voter a choice of *alternatives.*"
Alumna. One female graduate; the plural is *alumnae. Alumnus* means
    one male graduate; the plural is *alumni,* which also is the plural for a
    group including both men and women.
Amateur, for *novice.* A novice is a beginner; an amateur is one who
    works or plays for fun, not money; a *professional* works or plays for
    money. Because the professional is usually highly skilled, an amateur
    is sometimes complimented by being called "professional."
Amused, See *bemused.*
And etc. Etc. stands for *et cetera,* which means "and the rest" in Latin,
    so the "and" is redundant.
Anxious, for *eager.* "He was *eager* [not *anxious*] to try, but his mother
    was *anxious* for his safety."
Ask. In its varied forms it can often be dropped. *"Asked* what he
    thought about the game, he said he thought it was good" can be
    simply "He said he thought the game was good."

Author, as a verb. "He *authored* a text" should be "He wrote a text."

Baby girl (or boy) *is born.* Redundant, as no one is born fully grown.

Badly injured. No injury is good; say "severely injured."

Beautiful. The word involves a value judgment, and some crank is bound to disagree, especially over a "beautiful woman."

Bemused, for *amused.* Bemused means dazed, preoccupied, or confused.

Boat, for *ship.* Technically, boats are carried on ships; generally, a boat is a small vessel.

Bridegroom. See *groom.*

Broadcasted, as the past tense of *broadcast.* "The program was *broadcast* daily."

Brutal beating. No beating is gentle.

Collide. This verb refers to a bumping of two moving objects. "The car hit [not *collided with*] a telephone pole and then *collided* with another car."

Complected or *complexioned.* The noun *complexion* has no adjective form. "She is fair *complected* [or *complexioned*]" should be "She has a fair *complexion.*"

Completely destroyed. The "completely" is redundant.

Comprise means contain, embrace, or include. The whole *comprises* the parts.

Consensus of opinion. "of opinion" is redundant, as a consensus is a collective opinion.

Controversial usually is a waste word. "The crowd shouted down the controversial proposal" can be simply "The crowd shouted down the proposal."

Contusion. See *laceration.*

Critical, for *critical condition.* A sick person in *critical condition* is seldom *critical.*

Currently. Usually redundant if the sentence is in the present tense. "He is *currently* appearing in *Macbeth*" can be simply "He is appearing in *Macbeth.*"

Devout, for *religious. Devout* is an exceptionally high degree of devotion—too high for the layman to measure.

Different than, for *different from.* "Each house is *different from* [not *different than*] the one next to it."

Dove, for *dived. Dove* is the colloquial, not the written, past tense of *dive.* "He *dived* [not *dove*] from the side of the boat."

Due to, for *because.* "He was late *because* [not *due to*] the battery went dead. He had been *due to* meet us at noon."

Eager. See *anxious.*

Elderly. Be cautious about this word, as even persons of seventy-five may be sensitive about being called *elderly.*

Esquire, the honorable, and other undefinable titles should be omitted.

Etc. See *and etc.*

Fewer. See *less.*

Foreseeable future. Who can see into the future?

Forgotten. See *gotten.*

For the purposes of can be simply *for.*

Freak accident is a cliché. Let the facts show that it is peculiar.

Gauntlet, for *gantlet.* A *gauntlet* is a glove and can be thrown down; a *gantlet* is a form of punishment and can be run.

Gotten, for *got. Gotten* is the colloquial past participle of *get,* but *forgotten* is the regular past participle of *forget.* "He had *got* the man's address but had *forgotten* to get his age."

Groom, for *bridegroom.* "The *bridegroom* had recently been employed as a *groom* with Smith Stables."

Ground rules. Except in reference to baseball games, skip the "ground."

Half mast, for *half staff.* Flags may fly at half mast on a ship but at *half staff* ashore.

Hung, for *hanged.* "Spectators *hung* over the wall to see the murderer *hanged.*"

Inform. See *advise.*

Jewish rabbis. Rabbi is Jewish by definition.

Laceration, for *contusion.* A *laceration* is a cut; a *contusion* is a bruise.

Ladies, for *women.* All *ladies* are women, but not all *women* are ladies. So call all women *women.*

Less, for *fewer. Less* refers to a general quantity; *fewer* refers to the specific items that make it up. "*Fewer* dollars earned means *less* money to spend."

Located, for *situated. Located* means "found," and *situated* means "placed at." "He *located* the school, which was *situated* five miles from town." As in this example, even "situated" can often be dropped without loss of meaning.

Majority, for *plurality.* In an election, a *majority* is more than half the votes, and the *plurality* is the margin of victory. "Jones was elected by a clear *majority* (64%), rolling up a *plurality* of 115,000 votes."

Media, for *medium. Media* is the plural of *medium.* "Television is an important *medium* for a political candidate today."

Militant, for mere *protestor* or for *rowdy.* A militant is a fighter for a cause; a rowdy fights for selfish reasons. A *protestor* may be against violence entirely.

Monies, for *money. Money* is collective, so the plural is unnecessary.

More unique or *most unique. Unique* is an absolute, so cannot be modified.

Novice. See *amateur.*

Orientated, for *oriented. Oriented* is the proper past tense of *orient.*

Panic, riot, disaster, etc. should not be used unless the facts clearly indicate the need for strong words.

Per (in *per year, per day,* etc.). Skip the Latin; use *a* year, *a* day. *Per annum* is doubly unfortunate.

Plurality. See *majority.*

Presently, for *now. Presently* is a long word meaning *soon.*

Prior to should be simply *before.*

Professional. See *amateur.*

Protestor. See *militant.*

Raised, for *reared.* Children are *reared;* animals are *raised.*

Reason why is redundant.

Red-headed, for *red-haired.* Be accurate. Do you mean the scalp or the hair?

Religious. See *devout.*

Resides is a fancy way of saying *lives.*

Revert back is redundant.

Rowdy. See *militant.*

Ship. See *boat.*

Situated. See *located.*

Sudden explosion is redundant.

Superlatives (like eldest, fastest, biggest) should be handled with care. Often someone will be challenged to find something that surpasses your example.

The before a plural noun is usually unnecessary. "The voters filled the polling booths" could be simply "Voters filled the polling booths." Let your ear be your guide.

These kind should be *these kinds.*

Thusly should be *thus.*

To death is often redundant, as in "strangled to death" or "drowned to death."

Unaware of the fact that should be simply "unaware that."

Utterly, flatly, sheer, categorically, definitely, and many other such adverbs only pad most sentences.

Very should be used very seldom.

Whether or not, for *whether.* Because it implies an alternative, *whether* rarely needs to be followed by *or not.*

Wise is a bad general suffix. Other*wise* is fine, but health*wise*, automobile*wise*, tax*wise*, etc. smack too much of advertising shoptalk.

Grammar

Journalists often need review of these grammatical points.*

About may indicate approximation; *around* implies motion. "He weighs *about* 150 pounds and runs two miles *around* the track each day."

Adjective phrases should be hyphenated. "The *2-year-old* boy ran to the *sad-looking* man.

---

* Adapted from a section in *High School Journalism Today,* Gene Gilmore, ed. (Danville, Ill.: Interstate Publishers), 1967.

Adjectives referring to health or emotion. See *feel.*

Affect is a verb and means *to have influence. Effect,* as a noun, refers to a result. "His speech *affected* the audience deeply; the *effect* was a silence so profound one could hear the crickets outside the tent." As a verb, *effect* means *to bring about* or *accomplish.* "His work *effected* a cure." Note that as a verb *effect* is usually unnecessary. "His work cured her."

Agreement. A subject and its predicate, and a noun and its pronoun, should agree in number. "The *group* of boys *was* trying to break down the door. The *girls* inside *were* screaming in panic. The *group* lost *its* steam when the dean appeared and told the *boys* he had called *their* parents."

Among. See *between.*

Apostrophe (to indicate possession). See *possessives.*

Around. See *about.*

As. See *like.*

Beside refers to nearness; *besides* means *in addition to.* "*Besides* being sheriff he was dog catcher, so he built the dog pound *beside* the jail."

Between refers to two persons or things; *among* refers to three or more. "The power of government is divided *among* the legislative, judicial, and executive branches. The legislative power is divided *between* the Senate and the House."

Capitalization (in quotations). See *quotations.*

Commas setting off appositives or interrupters come in pairs. "John Smith, senator from Vermont will speak today" should be "John Smith, senator from Vermont, will speak today." And "The meeting, surprisingly enough went off on schedule" needs a comma after "enough."

Contrary-to-fact statements. See *subjunctive mood.*

Doubt, statements of. See *subjunctive mood.*

Effect. See *affect.*

Either pairs with *or; neither* pairs with *nor.* "*Either* he *or* I is at fault, but *neither* he *nor* I admits guilt." Note that both *either* and *neither* require singular verbs.

Farther refers to distance; *further* refers to thoroughness. "He wanted to check *further* on the flood damage, so he walked *farther* out onto the bridge."

Feel, when it refers to health or emotion, requires an adjective, not an adverb. "I feel bad about not calling him back." "I feel badly" would imply an impaired sense of touch. The same rule applies to *look, sound, smell,* and *taste.*

Gerunds coupled with a pronoun require that pronoun to be possessive. "I could watch *his dancing* for hours."

Hyphenation, of adjective phrases. See *adjective phrases.*

It's and *its. It's* is a contraction of *it is; its* is a possessive pronoun. "*It's* too bad the store lost *its* lease."

Lay and *lie.* To *lay* is a transitive verb and thereby takes an object; *to lie* is intransitive and thus takes no object.

Transitive: He *lays* bricks for a living.
He is *laying* the box on the counter.
Lay the box on the counter.
He *laid* the box down.

Intransitive: He *lies* in bed till noon.
He is *lying* in the sun.
Lie down for an hour or so.
He *lay* down to rest.
His head *lay* on the pillow.
He has *lain* there long enough.

Like is a preposition and requires an object; *as* is a conjunction and requires a following clause. "She looks *like* her mother, just *as* [not *like*] we thought." *Like* may be used as a conjunction in a simile. "He performed *like* Artur Rubinstein."
Look, when referring to health. See *feel.*

Neither. See *either.*
Nor. See *either.*

Or. See *either.*

Possessives. To form the singular possessive, in most cases, add an apostrophe and an "s." "The dog's coat is glossy." To form a plural possessive, in most cases, add the apostrophe. "The dogs' coats are wet." If a word ends with an "s" sound, add only the apostrophe if it has more than one syllable. "Rabinowitz' book is well-written; Ross's book is dull."
Prepositional object. When a pronoun is the object of a preposition, it should be in the objective case. "The decision was between *him* and *me.*"

Quotations.
A quoted sentence needs only one capital:
"It is a difficult problem," Smith said, "but we can solve it."
Two quoted sentences require two capitals:
"The well is dry," she said. "We must get water elsewhere."
A quote within a quote takes single quotation marks:
"New devices let people 'hear' atomic explosions thousands of miles away," he said.
When quoted material continues for more than one paragraph, save the *ending* quotation marks for the end of the quoted material:
"The well is dry," she said; "we must get it elsewhere (no quotation marks).
"Maybe we can get it at the next farm."

Set and *sit.* To *set* is a transitive verb and thereby takes an object; *to sit* is intransitive and thus takes no object.

Transitive: He *sets* tile for a living.
He is *setting* plants in the garden.
Set the box on the table.
He *set* the box down.

Intransitive: He *sits* here regularly.
She was *sitting* in the chair.
Sit down, please.
He *sat* in front.
Have you *sat* there before?

Smell. See *feel.*
Sound. See *feel.*
Subjunctive mood. The subjunctive mood expresses wishes, doubts, or things contrary to fact. It requires a plural verb. "If he *were* seven feet tall, he would be on the basketball team for sure" (contrary to fact). "I wish I *were* old enough to be President" (wish). "He acts as if he *were* unable to speak" (doubt).

Taste. See *feel.*
Touch. See *feel.*

Were. See *subjunctive mood.*

Reporters often misspell or confuse these words:

Spelling

accommodate	flew, flu, flue	privilege
advice, advise	floe, flow	rhythm
allege	guerrilla	separate
amateur	hemorrhage	sergeant
arctic	judgment	sizable
bridal, bridle	knowledgeable	soccer
calendar	lessen, lesson	sophomore
canceled	libel, liable	stationary,
canvas, canvass	lose, loose	stationery
capital, capitol	mantel, mantle	there, their
category	mileage	weird.
cellar	missile	
cemetery	Niagara	
chauffeur	nickel	
cite, site, sight	ordinance, ordnance	
compliment,	peaceable	
complement	penitentiary	
conscious	personal, personnel	
coroner	Philippines	
corps, corpse	plaque	
council, counsel	prairie	
defendant	precede, proceed	
desert, dessert	preventive	
emigrate, immigrate	principal, principle	

Appendix b: glossary

ABC. Audit Bureau of Circulations, which compiles statistics on *circulations.*

Ad alley. A section of the *composing room* for *makeup* of ads.

Add. The copy added to a story; also, one *take* or page of a story, such as "Add 1."

Ad side. The section of the business office where advertising is prepared; sometimes a synonym for *ad alley.*

Advance. A story written in advance of an event and held for *release;* also, a story written on a forthcoming event.

Agate. Five-and-a-half-*point* type, usually found only in classified advertising or lists.

Agate line. A measurement of advertising depth. Fourteen make one inch.

Air. See *white space.*

Alive. Usable copy or type.

Alley. A section of the *composing room.* See *ad alley.*

All in hand. The situation when all copy has been sent to the *composing room.* All pages for the *edition* are *closed* and "ready to roll."

All up. The situation when the *copyeditor* or reporter has finished his assigned work. The copy is all in type.

AM. A morning newspaper. AMs is the cycle sent by a wire service to morning newspapers.

A-matter. Copy set in advance of the *top* of a story, sometimes called *10-add* material because it is added to *lead* paragraphs of a story.

ANPA. American Newspaper Publishers Association.

APC. Wire service jargon for "appreciate."

Art. Any illustrative material, such as pictures, graphs, and sketches.

Ascender. The portion of a *lower case* letter rising above average letter height; contrast to *descender.*

ASNE. American Society of Newspaper Editors.

Astonisher. An exclamation point.

Audience research. The study of newspaper readers—their education, wealth, etc.

Back room. The *composing room;* usually on smaller papers where it adjoins the news room. Also called back shop.

Back shop. See *back room.*

Bad break. An unattractive or confusing division of type in a story of more than one column. A column may end with a period, giving the impression that the story has ended, or there may be a prominent *widow.*

Balloon. A device used in comic strips to make words appear to come from a character.

Bank. A part of a headline, sometimes called a deck or, if the lower part, a drop. It also means a storage place for stories or ads set in type.

Banner. A headline running across, or nearly across, the top of a page; also called streamer, line, ribbon.

Bastard type. Type that differs from the standard *point* system.

Beat. The area assigned to a reporter for his regular coverage—his run; also, an exclusive story, or scoop.

Ben Day. An *engraving* process that provides shading effects in line engravings. Editors use Ben Day mostly for borders on key stories.

BF. The abbreviation for *boldface.*

Binder. A small *banner* across an inside page. It sometimes shelters several related stories.

Bite. To cut a story so it fits the space allotted to it. The part cut is called a biteoff or a bite.

Biteoff. See *bite.*

Blanket. See *offset.*

Bleed. To run a *cut* right off the edge of a page; also, the cut so run. Sometimes a cut run to the edge of the outside column is erroneously called a bleed.

Blind ad. A classified ad which gives a box number instead of the advertiser's name.

Blind interview. An interview story which does not reveal the name of the source, referring to him as "an informed official," "an unimpeachable source," etc.

Blotter. A police department's record book.

Blow up. To enlarge printed or pictorial matter; the enlargement so made.

Body. The story itself, as distinguished from the headline and the illustration.

Body type. The type normally used for news stories. The size is usually 8-, 9-, or 10-*point.*

Boil or *boil down.* A *copyeditor*'s direction to reduce a story substantially.

Boiler plate. Editorial matter, usually *features* and pictures, mailed to small papers in *matrix* or metallic form.

Boldface. Dark or heavy type, as distinguished from *lightface;* sometimes called fullface. **This is boldface.**

Book. A group of several stories on the same general subject, usually from a wire service. See also *take.*

Border. The strips of type metal surrounding an ad, story, or headline.

Box. To enclose a story or headline with four *rules* to give it more prominence; also, such an enclosure.

Box-all. The instruction to put the headline, *body,* and, possibly, picture of a story in a single *box.*

Break. The division of a story continued from one page to another or from one column to another. Compare *jump, bad break, break-over, wrap, carryover.* Also, a story breaks when the event occurs or when the news becomes available to reporters.

Break-over. The part of a story continued to another page. The page where break-overs are placed is called the break-over page, carryover, or jump page.

Brite. A short, amusing feature story; short for page brightener.

Budget. The listing of stories expected by a wire service or by another news gathering group; also called news digest.

Bug. Any fancy typographic device used to break up areas of type, especially in headlines. Compare *dingbat*. Bugs are used with restraint by today's editors. The word also refers to the telegrapher's key and to the label of the International Typographical Union.

Bulldog. The newspaper's first *edition* of the day.

Bullet. A large black dot used for decoration, to separate sections of a story, or, at the left edge of a column, to mark each item in a series.

Bulletin. Important and often unexpected news. In wire service parlance only a *flash* is more important.

Bulletin-form. A wire service term for filing a story in short installments, or *takes*.

Bulletin precede. The latest facts of a story already set in type when the bulletin arrived. The precede is stuck in at the top of the story.

Bureau. A subsidiary newsgathering force placed in a smaller community, a state capital, or the national capital by a newspaper or wire service.

Business-office must. A story labeled "must" by the business office, which means the story cannot be omitted. Usually it is a page-one *box* promoting the paper itself.

C and lc. The abbreviation for *caps and lower case,* used to specify the conventional capitalizing used in ordinary writing; contrast to material marked "caps," which means the compositor should set every letter as a capital.

C and sc. The abbreviation for *caps and small caps,* used to set material all in capitals but with the pattern of *C and lc.*

Cablese. See *skeletonize*.

Canned copy. Prepared news or editorials sent by a *syndicate* or publicity organization.

Caps. The abbreviation for capitals; also, upper case. Every letter or a word so marked is capitalized. Compare *C and lc* and *C and sc.*

Caption. A headline appearing above a picture; now, through misuse, commonly a synonym for *cutline,* the words under a picture.

Carryover. See *break-over.*

Casting. A *plate,* usually an ad or picture, made by pouring molten type metal over a papier mâché *matrix.*

Casting box. The equipment used to cast a printing *plate* from a papier mâché *matrix.*

Catchline. See *guideline.*

Center. To place type in the center of a line.

CGO. Short for *can go over.* Copy that could be held for another day.

Chapel. A union local for printers, stereotypers, or pressmen.

Chase. A frame in which type is placed to make a page *form.*

Chi square. A test of statistical validity; used in communicatons research.

Circulation. The number of copies a paper sells in a particular *edition;* the department in charge of distributing the paper.

Circus makeup. A now rare *makeup* system which uses many large headlines scattered seemingly as random on a page.

City desk. The place where the city editor and his assistants, if any, work.

City editor. The editor in charge of the reporters covering news within a city and its environs. On smaller papers he also edits his reporters' copy.

City room. The news room, where reporters and editors work.

Clean copy. A story needing little editing.

Clean proof. A *proof* needing few corrections.

Clipsheet. A sheet of publicity material which its backers hope will be clipped and reprinted. AP and UPI, however, send filler material on a clipsheet.

Closed. A page *locked up,* ready for *stereotyping* and therefore not to be altered except in an emergency.

Col. The abbreviation for column.

Cold type. Print produced photographically or by a machine resembling a typewriter. Strips of paper so "printed" are pasted on a *dummy* and photographed, and a *plate* for an *offset* press is made from the negative.

Color. A story with human interest, often describing places and people in detail. But a "colored" story is a biased, or slanted, report.

Column inch. One inch of type one column wide; a standard measure of advertising space for smaller papers.

Column rule. A thin line separating columns.

Communicologist. A communications researcher; often used in derision.

Compose. To set type. See *compositor.*

Composing room. The mechanical department; in particular the place where type is *composed* and put into *forms.*

Composing stick. The small metal tray in which a *compositor* arranges type he is setting by hand.

Compositor. Someone who sets type professionally, either by hand or by machine.

Condensed type. Type narrower than the standard width of a particular type *face,* giving a squeezed appearance; contrast *extended type.*

Content analysis. A research method to analyze published material.

Copy boy. An errand boy in the news room. "Copy girls" perform the same duties.

Copy cutter. A *composing room* worker who cuts copy into various *takes* to facilitate quick typesetting. He also distributes copy to various *Linotype* operators.

Copydesk. A desk, frequently horseshoe-shaped, around which *copy-editors* sit to edit copy. The *slot man,* inside the horseshoe, is in charge.

Copyeditor. A person who edits copy; a copyreader.

Copyreader. See *copyeditor.*

Copy writer. A person who writes advertising copy.

Correspondent. A reporter who files stories from places outside the newspaper's city area. He may be on salary or may receive a flat fee or a per-inch rate. See also *stringer.*

Country copy. News from rural areas, often written by a part-time *correspondent*, or *stringer.*

CQ. An abbreviation for "correct"; used in copy but not as a symbol on *proof* or on a *mark.* See also *CX.*

Credit line. A line acknowledging the source for a story or picture.

Crop. To cut away parts of a picture to eliminate unwanted material or to make it a particular size.

Cut. To reduce a story's length; compare *bite.* As a noun, an *engraving* and therefore any *art.*

Cutline. Any explanatory material under a piece of *art.* Compare *caption.*

Cutoff rule. A horizontal line, the width of a column, used to separate material.

CX. An abbreviation for "correct." The editor puts this symbol on *proof* corrected in the newsroom, or on a *mark.* The symbols "X-correct" and "Krect" are also used for this purpose. All three abbreviations are used on edited copy to show the typesetter that something that might seem wrong is right. See also *CQ.*

Dateline. The words that give the story's origin and, often, the date on which the story was written, e.g., CHICAGO, Oct. 1 (UPI)–.

Dayside. The shift of day workers in the news room.

Dead. Copy or type that will not be used.

Dead bank. A storage area for *dead* type.

Dead stone. See *dead bank.*

Deck. See *bank.*

Descender. The portion of a *lower case* letter going below the baseline; contrast *ascender.*

Desk chief. The head of a particular desk.

Dingbat. Any typographical device used for decoration. Compare *bug.*

Dinky dash. A short dash used to separate items in a series.

Dirty copy. Matter for publication which is sloppy, full of corrections, and badly marked up; contrast to *clean copy.*

Display ad. All advertising except classified and legal.

District man. A reporter covering a particular district of a city or rural area.

Dog watch. See *lobster trick.*

Dope story. An interpretative story often based on background plus speculation.

Doublet. The repetition of some fact; also called doubleton.

Doubleton. See *doublet.*

Double-truck. A two-page layout, either news or advertising, which eliminates the margin, or *gutter,* between the pages.

Downstyle. A style with a minimum of capitalization. Contrast *upstyle.*

DPR. The telegraph symbol for Day Press Rate.

Drop. See *bank.*

Drop head. A headline with each line stepped (and so also called a step head):

President Says
Budget Deficit
Above Estimate

Drop line. See *drop head.*

Dummy. A diagram of a newspaper page used to show printers where stories, pictures, and ads are to be placed; occasionally called a map.

Dupe. A duplicate, usually a carbon copy; also, a story that appears twice in the same *edition.*

Ear. Either upper corner of the front page, often containing a slogan or a weather report.

Edition. Each *run* of a newspaper *issue.* There may be market editions, early editions, final editions, etc.

Editorial. Generally all the non-advertising and non-business material or operations of a newspaper; also, one of the opinion essays of the editorial page.

Electrotype. A copper-plated reproduction of type or *art;* usually used in advertising or book publishing.

Em. The square of the type size. An em in 12-*point* type is twelve points high and twelve points wide. Sometimes erroneously used to mean one-sixth of an inch; see *pica.*

En. Half an *em.*

End dash. A dash at the end of a story; usually about six *picas.* It is sometimes called a thirty-dash.

Engraving. A *plate* from which pictures and drawings may be printed; see *cut.*

Etaoin shrdlu. A *Linotype* operator sets these "words" to fill out a line he plans to throw away. The letters make up the first two vertical rows on a *Linotype.*

Exchange. A copy of a newspaper sent to another newspaper publisher as part of an agreement to exchange subscriptions.

Extended type. Type wider than the standard for a particular *face;* contrast *condensed type.*

Extra. A special, or extra, *edition* published because of spectacular news; now rare.

Eye camera. A camera specially arranged to record a reader's eye movements; used in research on *makeup.*

Face. A particular design of type; also, the printing surface of type.

Fake. A false story.

Feature. A story emphasizing the human interest or entertainment aspects of a situation; usually in narrative form. Also, material such as columns and comics brought from a *syndicate.* As a verb, it means to give prominence to a story; to emphasize a part of a story.

FF or *ff.* The abbreviation for fullface. See *boldface.*

File. To transmit a story by telephone, telegraph, or cable. As a noun, it refers collectively to the back issues of a paper; also, one day's production by a wire service.

Filler. Short stories, usually *time copy,* used to fill small spaces in the
paper.

Fingernails. Parentheses; sometimes called toenails.

First-day story. The first published account of an event.

Flag. The newspaper's *nameplate* or *logotype,* often erroneously called
the *masthead;* also, a *slug* or piece of paper inserted into printing
forms to remind printers that a correction, *add,* or *insert* is required
at that point.

Flash. The highest priority of news sent by a wire service; used rarely.

Flat-bed press. A press which prints from a flat surface.

Flimsy. Thin paper used for carbon copies; sometimes the carbon copy
itself.

Flong. A cardboard-like sheet used for making the *matrix* in *stereotyping.*

Fluff. Inconsequential material.

Flush. The instructions to set type even, or flush, with a margin; "flush
left" means flush with the left margin, "flush right" with the right
margin.

Flush head. A headline whose lines are even on the left:

President Says
Budget Plan
'Unrealistic'

Folio. The line at the top of the page giving the page number, the name
of the newspaper, the city of publication, and the date; also, a measure for legal advertising.

Follow. A story that *follows up* a *first-day* story; also, a *second-day*
story; also, a story *shirt-tailed* to a similar, but more important,
story.

Follow up. A story that gives the latest news of an event reported
earlier.

Folo. An abbreviation for *follow.* Also see *folo copy.*

Folo copy. The order to set copy in type exactly as written.

Font. A set of a particular size and style of type.

Form. A *chase* filled with type.

Format. The physical appearance of a page, section, or book.

Four-color process. A printing process using four different engraving
plates, each printing one color—black, red, blue, or yellow—to make
natural-looking color.

Fourth estate. The public press.

Front office. The business office.

Fudge. A part of a press *plate* that may be removed or chiseled away so
last-minute news, usually sports scores, can be inserted; also called a
fudge box.

Fullface. See *boldface.*

Full line. Type that fills the line, making it both *flush* left and flush
right; a line that has no room for spacing.

Future. A reminder of a forthcoming event. Such notes are put in a
"future book" to be used in making reporting assignments. "Futures" are stories to be used within a few days or weeks.

FYI. The wire service abbreviation for "for your information."

Galley. A metal tray to hold type; also, about twenty inches of type.

Galley proof. A *proof* of a *galley* of type; used to check the copy for errors before it goes to press.

Ghost. A ghost writer; a person who writes stories or books for others' signatures.

Glossy. A shiny-surfaced photograph, best suited for *photoengraving.*

Goodnight. A wire service may end its *AMs* cycle with this word; an editor may call it out to a staffer, thereby indicating the staffer may leave for the day.

Graf. Short for paragraph.

Graveyard shift. The work period that covers the early morning hours; also called *lobster trick* or *dog watch.* Staffers on this shift may write and edit, but they are there primarily to cover emergencies.

Gravure. A process for printing from an indented surface. See also *intaglio* and *rotogravure.*

Gray out. A section of a page that has no typographical contrast, giving a gray appearance.

Green eyeshade. A somewhat sentimental term for an old-time newspaperman; refers to a former custom among deskmen of wearing green eyeshades.

Guideline. The first word or two of a headline, written at the top of the copy to identify it; also called catchline. It is sometimes confused with *slugline.*

Gutter. The margin between facing pages.

Hairline. An extra-thin *rule.*

Halftone. An engraving using small dots of varying depth to produce shaded effects, as in photos; contrast to *line cut.*

Handout. A press release.

Handset. Type set by hand.

Hanging indent. A headline with first line set flush left and other lines slightly and equally indented:

President Says
Budget Plan
'Unrealistic'

Head. Short for headline.

Head schedule. A sheet that displays headline types used by the newspaper; it includes the unit count for each type face so the editor can quickly figure how much space a word will take up in the headline. Popularly called the "hed sked."

Head slug. A *slug* which does not print, separating the headline from the story with blank space.

Head to come. The notice to the composing room that the headline will be sent after the story; abbreviated HTK or HTC.

Headwriter. A writer of headlines; usually a *copyeditor,* who writes the headlines for the story he edits.

Hed sked. Short for *head schedule.*

Hellbox. A container in the *composing room* for unwanted type.

Holdover. See *overset.*

Hole. See *news hole.*

House organ. A publication issued by a company primarily for its employees.

HTC or HTK. Abbreviations for *head to come.*

Human interest. The quality giving a story wide appeal. It often contains information on human foibles or oddities or heartwarming and sentimental matter.

Index. The summary of the contents or highlights of a paper; usually on page one.

Initial. A large capital letter at the beginning of an article or paragraph, common in magazines but sometimes used for magazine-style matter in newspapers.

Insert. Copy or type to be inserted into a story.

Intaglio printing. The *gravure* process that prints ink from a depressed surface.

Inverted pyramid. A headline form with each line centered and shorter than the preceding one:

**President Reports
Deficit Plan
Today**

Also, a news story with facts arranged in descending order of importance.

Issue. One day's newspaper, which may have several *editions.*

Ital. or itals. Abbreviations for *italics.*

Italics. Type with letters slanted to the right; used for cross references in this glossary. Contrast *roman* and *oblique.*

ITU. International Typographical Union, to which most printers (but not stereotypers or pressmen) belong.

Jim dash. A dash about three *picas* long, often used to separate a regular story and a *shirttail.*

Job. A commercial printing order.

Job press. A press used only for commercial printing.

Jump. See *break-over;* also, to continue a story. Compare *break.*

Jump head. The headline over the part of the story that was continued, or *jumped,* to another page.

Jump line. A line noting a story is continued (e.g., *Continued on Page 6*).

Jump page. See *break-over.*

Justify. To space out a column to make the type snug, or to space out a line of type so it is *flush* left and right.

Justowriter. A machine, basically like a typewriter, which sets *cold type.*

Kicker. A few words usually to the left and above a headline, to give it emphasis; sometimes it serves the same purpose as a *deck.*

Kill. To eliminate all or part of a story. Compare *mandatory kill.*

Label head. A headline, usually without a verb, that only labels the news and thus is listless (e.g., *List of Graduates*).

Late watch. See *lobster trick.*

Layout. A planned arrangement of stories and pictures on one subject; also, the whole typographical arrangement of a newspaper.

LC or *lc.* Abbreviations for *lower case.*

Lead (pronounced "led"). A strip of metal used to separate *slugs* of type. Strips are placed between paragraphs to justify a column.

Lead (pronounced "leed"). The first paragraph or two of a story; also, the story given number one position as the best of the day. Also, a *tip.*

Lead ("leed") *editorial.* The first, and most important, editorial.

Lead ("leed") *to come.* A device, used rarely, to indicate that the story's *lead* will come later. Compare *ten-add.*

Leaders ("leeders"). Dots or dashes to take the eye across a column; often used in tables.

Leftover. See *overset.*

Leg man. A reporter who gathers information and telephones it to a *rewrite man.*

Legibility. The quality of a type style which makes it easily and quickly comprehended or perceived; contrast *readability.*

Letterpress printing. The process by which ink is transferred to paper from a raised surface; the traditional method of printing.

Letter space. The insertion of thin spaces between letters to *justify* the line.

Library. A collection of clippings, newspaper files, and reference books; formerly called the morgue.

Ligature. One character of type that includes more than one letter (e.g., *fl* and œ). The initials of the wire services, such as AP and UPI, are also known as ligatures.

Linage. A measure of printed material based on the number of lines; also, the total amount of advertising over a given period of time.

Line. See *banner;* also, *agate line.*

Linecasting machine. A machine that casts line of type. Compare *Linotype.*

Line cut. An engraving which prints only black and white; also called line engraving. Contrast *halftone.*

Line gauge. A printer's ruler.

Lino. Short for *Linotype.*

Linotype. The brand name of a machine which sets hot type one line at a time; also a loose term for all similar machines.

Lithography. The process of printing from ink impressed on a sheet; also called photolithography. See also *offset.*

Live. Designation for type that will be used in the paper going to press.

Lobster trick. The shift on duty after the last *edition* of a morning paper has gone to press; the night shift of an afternoon paper. Sometimes called lobster shift, late watch, and dog watch. See also *graveyard shift* and *nightside.*

Local. A local news item; usually a *personal.*

Localize. To emphasize a local angle in a story.

Locked up. See *closed.*

Log or *logo.* Short for *logotype.*

Logotype. A one-piece line of type or a *plate* bearing a trademark, name, or frequently used phrase. A newspaper's *nameplate,* or *flag,* is a logotype.

Lower case. The small letters of type. The term originated with early type cases, which had the small letters near the bottom. Contrast *upper case.* See also *downstyle.*

Ludlow. A typecasting machine used for headlines or advertising. It casts *slugs* from *matrices* that are *handset.*

Magazine. An attachment on a *linecasting machine* for the storing of *matrices.*

Magazine style. See *upstyle;* also see *initial.*

Mail edition. An *edition* sent primarily to mail subscribers.

Makeover. To make a new page *plate* to correct an error or to include late news; also called replate.

Makeready. The series of *composing room* processes that prepare material for printing.

Makeup. To arrange type and pictures to produce a desired effect. The noun refers to the resulting design.

Makeup editor. An editorial employee stationed in the *composing room* to supervise the *makeup* of the paper.

Makeup rule. A thin piece of steel, shaped something like a protractor, used by printers in page *makeup.*

Mandatory kill. An order from a wire service to eliminate (*kill*) a story, probably because it has a serious error or is libelous.

Map. See *dummy.*

Mark. A story from one *edition* clipped and pasted on a sheet of paper to be marked for changes in the next edition—corrections, indications of inserts, adds, or new leads. Also called a markup or marker.

Marker. See *mark.*

Markets. A section of the paper that includes news of livestock, commodity, and stock markets.

Markup. See *mark.*

Masthead. A statement of the paper's name, ownership, subscription rate, etc., which often appears on the editorial page; often confused with *nameplate* or *flag.*

Mat. Short for *matrix.*

Matrix (plural: matrices). A die or mold from which type is cast. It can be papier mâché, from which the page *plate* is cast, or a brass die, from which lines of type are cast. Commonly referred to as mat.

Mat roller. The machine which squeezes the papier mâché matrix against the *form,* preparatory to making a page *plate.*

Measure. The length of a line of type, or the width of a column.

Media Records, Inc. A company that records data on newspaper advertising.

Milline rate. A method of measuring advertising rates in relation to *circulation.*

Monotype. A typecasting machine that sets each letter in a separate piece of metal.

More. A word placed at the end of a sheet of copy to indicate that the story has not ended.

Morgue. See *library.*

Mortice. An opening, usually rectangular, for the insertion of material, such as an opening in an *engraving* for a heading.

Must. An order from a superior that a certain story must run in the paper that day. See also *business office must.*

Nameplate. The *logotype* that carries the newspaper's name at the top of page one; also called *flag* and, wrongly, *masthead.*

NANA. North American Newspaper Alliance, a news *syndicate* specializing in feature stories.

National advertising. Advertising placed by an advertising agency, usually for a product sold nationally.

NEA. National Editorial Association, a group of weekly and small-daily editors; also, Newspaper Enterprise Association, a *feature* service.

New lead (pronounced "leed"). Also called new top. A fresh opening paragraph or two for a story. An editor may think the reporter's story basically sound but in need of a new *lead* to catch the reader's interest. Or the story may have been published earlier and need a new beginning; see also *second-day story.*

News digest. See *budget.*

News hole. The space in a paper allotted to news reports and illustration, the rest being given to advertisements, comic strips, etc.

New top. See *new lead.*

Nightside. The night shift of a newspaper. See also *lobster trick.*

Nonpareil. Six-*point* type.

NPR. The telegraph symbol for Night Press Rate.

Nutted. Type indented one *en.*

Obit. Short for *obituary.*

Obituary. A story reporting a person's death. For a well-known person, it is often written before he dies; the facts of his death are simply incorporated into the pre-written story of his life.

Oblique type. Slanted type, but without the handwritten appearance of *italics.* Contrast *roman.*

Off its feet. Type that does not quite stand vertically and therefore makes a poor impression on the paper.

Offset. A photographic method of printing. Copy is photographed and a *plate* made by "burning" light through the negative onto a sensitized sheet of thin metal. The part exposed to light, or "burned," absorbs ink while the rest of the plate rejects it. The plate, wrapped around a roller, transfers, or offsets, the ink to a rubber roller called a blanket, which actually imprints the paper.

Op ed or *opp page.* Abbreviations for "the page opposite"; usually the page devoted to columns and *features* and placed opposite the editorial page.

Overset. Set type that cannot be used because space is filled; called holdover or leftover if it can be used in the next issue.

Page proof. A *proof* (test printing) of a full page. Such proofs often are taken of the front page before it is made into a *plate.*

Patent or *patent insides.* Pre-printed material, usually on one side of a sheet so local news can be printed on the blank side; used rarely now, even on the smallest weeklies. Also see *readyprint.*

Perforator. A machine used to perforate a paper tape from which type can be set mechanically; also, a person who runs a perforator.

Personal. A one-paragraph item about minor family news; a kind of *local.*

Photocomposition. A photographic process to "set type." Actually, letters are formed on film which is photographically printed; then that print is photographed in the *offset* process to make a *plate.*

Photoengraving. See *engraving.*

Photolithography. See *lithography.*

Pi. Jumbled type, or, as a verb, to jumble type; past tense or adjective form is "pied."

Pica. Twelve-*point* type; also, a printer's measure—one-sixth of an inch. It is also called *pica em* or, wrongly, *em.*

Pica em. See *pica.*

Pick up. The instruction at the bottom of copy to tell the printer to pick up other type and add it to the story. In wire copy, it tells the editor where *adds, inserts,* etc. "pick up" into the story.

Pix. Short for pictures.

Planer. A wooden block pounded against type in *form* to make it level.

Plate. A *stereotype* page or an *offset* metal sheet from which newspapers are printed.

Platen press. A small *job press.*

Play. The typographical emphasis given a story, or the emphasis on a certain fact in a story. Facts or stories can be "played up" or "played down."

PM. An afternoon newspaper.

Point. A type measurement—one seventy-second of an inch. Hence, 72-point type is one inch high, 36-point one-half inch, etc.

Policy. The newspaper's position on how it handles news.

Policy story. A story that supports the newspaper *policy.*

Poll. A field study of opinion on an issue. It may be a scientific *public opinion survey* or merely unscientific guesswork.

PR. Public relations.

Precede. A *new lead* or story, taking precedence over a previous wire service transmission and usually intended to precede it. A *bulletin precede* could be set in type and placed ahead of the earlier story.

Pre-date. An issue printed before its announced date of publication. (Metropolitan morning papers put out an *edition* in the evening with the next day's date on it.)

Preferred position. An advertising term that refers to an advertiser's receiving a special place in the paper for his ads. Usually the advertiser pays extra for this preference.

Press agent. A person hired to get favorable publicity for an individual or organization.

Process color. A printing method that mixes primary colors optically to produce a full range of colors.

Proof. A test impression taken from type set and ready for printing. It allows errors to be spotted and corrections made before the paper goes to press. See also *galley proof.*

Proof press. A simple press used to make *proof.*

Proofreader. An employee in the *composing room* who reads and marks *proof* to make sure it conforms to copy.

Public opinion survey. A scientific study of the expressed attitudes of a representative sample of a population; often used before elections.

Public relations. The craft of issuing news of and creating a good image for an individual, agency, or firm; more professional and comprehensive than the work of a *press agent.* Often shortened to PR.

Puff, puffery. A publicity story or a story that contains unwarranted superlatives.

Puncher. A *teletype* operator.

Put to bed. See *all in hand.*

Q. and A. Copy including question-and-answer material, as in court testimony or a long interview.

Query. A question raised in a message to a wire service; also, a request by a freelance writer to see if a newspaper or magazine would be interested in a particular article.

Railroad. To send copy to the *composing room* with little or no editing; to put type into *forms* without *proofreading.*

Readability. The quality of copy which makes it easy to grasp; contrast *legibility.*

Reader interest. A type of research to determine the degree of appeal different materials have for the reader.

Readership. Research on the amount of newspaper copy which readers notice or read; also, the people actually reached by a publication, as distinguished from *circulation.*

Readout. A subsidiary headline that "reads out" (explains in more detail) from a *banner.*

Readyprint. Paper already partly printed with ads and *features,* so the rest of the space can be filled with local news and ads. See also *patent.*

Register. The correct placement or matching of *plates* in color printing so colors are exactly where they should be.

Release. The date and time at which a news source says information may be released to the public; also, a publicity handout; also, authorization for the use of a photograph.

Replate. See *makeover.*

Reprint. Published material that came from a previous issue or from some other source, such as a magazine.

Reproduction proof or *repro proof.* A fine *proof* on quality paper for use in preparing a *plate,* as in *offset.*

Retail advertising. Advertising placed by local merchants.

Retouch. To change a photograph, usually to improve it for *engraving,* by painting sections out (or in) with a small brush.

Revamp. To alter a story by shifting some of the paragraphs, but not by rewriting it. See also *rewrite.*

Reverse. Letters or *engravings* printed the opposite of normal, as white letters on a black background.

Reverse-6. The eye tends to scan the news page in a line resembling a reversed number 6.

Revise. A second, and presumably correct, *proof*—made after errors were noted on the first proof.

Rewrite. To write a story again, or to *revamp* a story from a wire service or from another newspaper; also, to write a story telephoned to the news room by another reporter. See also *rewrite man.*

Rewrite man. The reporter who takes facts from one or more reporters, usually by telephone, and writes the story; also, a reporter who revises stories written by other reporters.

Ribbon. See *banner.*

Rim. The outside edge of the *copydesk,* which is traditionally horse-shoe-shaped.

Rim man. A *copyeditor,* so named because he sits on the *rim.*

Roman type. The common vertical type which is popularly contrasted to *italic* and technically to *oblique.*

ROP. Short for *run of paper.*

Roto. Short for *rotogravure.*

Rotogravure. An *intaglio* printing process using etching on copper and a rotary press; also, a section of a newspaper featuring photographs so printed.

Routing. Gouging metal from a *cut, casting,* or a page *plate* so only part of the surface will print.

Rule. A metal strip which prints a line dividing columns, stories, or sections of advertising; usually one or two *points* thick, but see also *hairline.*

Ruled insert. A story that accompanies another but is set off from it by *rules.*

Run. An *edition,* in the sense that the edition is "run"; also, a *beat.*

Run in. The instruction on copy to have material in tables or paragraphs run together without paragraphing.

Running story. A story—actually many stories—continued for several days or more.

Run of paper. An order meaning that an ad, picture, or story could go almost anyplace in the paper. Also, color printed by regular newspaper presses.

Sacred cow. A person or institution unethically deferred to by being given special news treatment.

Sans serif. See *serif.*

SAP. Occasionally used in messages to mean "soon as possible." The superlative SAPPEST is used humorously.

Schedule. A record of stories assigned or already processed.

Scoop. See *beat.*

Screen. A mesh through which pictures are rephotographed in making *engravings* or *cuts.* A fairly coarse screen is used in making newspaper cuts.

Second-day story. A story previously published but now carrying a *new lead* or some other revision to make it news. Also see *follow.*

Second front page. Usually the front page of a second section; also called split page. Sometimes page two or page three gets the name because it carries important news with little or no advertising.

Sectional story. A story received in pieces or sent to the *composing room* in sections; also, a story that would be of interest only to readers in a certain area.

See copy. The direction to *proofreaders* to check the *proof* against the copy.

Send down or *send out.* The direction to send copy to the *composing room.*

Separate. A story related to another and displayed separately, but usually nearby.

Series. Related stories, usually run on consecutive days.

Serif. A tiny finishing stroke or squiggle at the ends of letters in most type faces. A face with simple, square corners is called sans serif.

Set. To arrange type, either by hand or by machine, for printing.

Shirttail. Material added to a major story; also, a short *follow.*

Sidebar. A story that emphasizes one part of a main story and appears alongside it on the page.

Sidelight. A kind of *sidebar,* often dealing with a personality or one aspect of an event.

Side story. See *sidebar.*

Signature. An advertiser's name, often in distinctive type, in his ad; often printed from a *logotype.*

Skeletonize. To reduce copy by eliminating articles, some conjunctions, etc. in order to minimize cable tolls; now rarely done. The skeletonized language is called cablese.

Skyline. A line running above the *nameplate,* at the top of the page.

Slant. To emphasize a certain part or angle of a story; also, to distort the news. Compare *color.*

Slot. The inside of the horseshoe-shaped *copydesk;* occupied by the slot man, who directs the *copyeditors* sitting around the *rim.*

Slot man. See *slot.*

Slug or *slugline.* A mark on a story, usually one word like "blast" or "money," for identification as it passes through the news room and *composing room.*

Small caps. Capital letters smaller than the regular capitals of a particular type face; used almost exclusively in magazines and books, and rarely there. See also *C and sc.*

Soc. Short for society; sometimes "sox."

Solid. Lines of type set without space, or *lead,* between them.

Sox. See *soc.*

Space grabber. A publicity seeker.

Spike. A spindle, usually for unwanted copy; also, to eliminate, or *kill,* a story.

Split page. See *second front page.*

Split run. The dividing of a publication run into two or more slightly different versions, sometimes for research. For example, to check the effectiveness of a new ad, one version would have the new ad and one would have the old.

Spot news. Information about a specific, recent occurrence, as contrasted to a story about a trend or continually developing situation.

Spread. A prominent display, usually with *art.* Sometimes the large, multi-column head over the material is called a "spread head."

Squib. A short news item.

Standing. Material kept in type because often needed, such as a column heading or the *nameplate.* A headline used repeatedly, such as the head over baseball standings, is called a standing head or stet head.

State editor. The person who edits the news from the newspaper's *circulation* area outside the metropolitan region.

Step head. See *drop head.*

Stereotype. A cylindrical or semi-cylindrical *plate* of a page. A papier mâché *matrix* is squeezed against the original type to make a mold. Molten metal is poured over the mold to make the stereotype.

Stet. The abbreviation for "let it stand," written above crossed-out words to indicate that they should be set in type after all.

Stet head. See *standing.*

Stick. A rough measurement meaning about two inches of type. See also *composing stick.*

Stone. A metal- or marble-topped table for page *makeup.* See also *turtle.*

Straight matter. Regular editorial material set in *body type* without variations from convention.

Straight news. A story with only the bare facts, without *color* interpretation.

Streamer. See *banner.*

String. Newspaper clippings to be added up by or for a *stringer* to see how much he should be paid. The term comes from saving the clips on a string; as a verb it means to work as a stringer.

Stringer. A part-time reporter living outside the newspaper's central area. See also *correspondent.*

Style book or *style sheet.* A specific list of the conventions of spelling, abbreviation, punctuation, capitalization, etc. used by a particular newspaper or wire service.

Sub. A piece of copy that substitutes for something in a previous story.

Subhead. A headline, usually one line of *body type* in *boldface,* that appears every few paragraphs. It should describe the news in the paragraph or two following.

Symmetry. A style of page *makeup* that balances elements on the page so neither the top nor the bottom, the left nor the right, dominates.

Syndicate. A firm which sells and distributes columns, comics, *features,* and pictures. A wire service technically is a syndicate, but is rarely called by that name.

Tabloid. A newspaper half the size of a regular eight-column, twenty-one-inch newspaper. The dimensions usually are five columns by sixteen inches. Though some "tabs" are sensational, the term is not a synonym for *yellow journalism.*

Take. A section of copy, usually a page long, sent to the *copydesk* or to the *composing room.* See also *book.*

Tear sheet. A newspaper page sent to an advertiser as evidence that his ad was printed.

Telegraph editor. The person who supervises the editing of news from wire services; thus often called the wire editor.

Teleprinter. See *teletype.*

Teletype. A machine that automatically types out news coming from a wire service; also called teleprinter and ticker. It can be used to transmit, as well as receive, news.

Teletypesetter. An attachment to a *Linotype* so it can set type from a perforated tape; commonly referred to as TTS.

Ten-add. A method for sending details of a story to the *composing room* before sending the *lead.* The initial piece of copy (*take*) is labeled 10-add, the next 11-add, etc.

Think piece. An interpretative article.

Thirty. The end of a story; written "30."

Thirty-dash. See *end dash.*

Thumbnail. A *cut* half a column wide.

Ticker. See *teletype.*

Tie-back. A reference in a story to some previous event—to help the reader's memory.

Tie-in. A story or part of a story linked to some other event.

Tight. A situation of little or no room in the whole paper, in a particular story, or in a line. See also *tight line.*

Tight line. A line too crowded for proper spacing between words.

Time copy. Material always current and therefore timeless; can be run whenever convenient.

Tip. Information that may lead to a story.

Toenails. See *fingernails.*

Tombstone. To place similar headlines side by side so the reader tends to read from head to head rather than from head to story.

Top. The first few paragraphs of a story.

Top deck. The main part of a headline.

TR. The abbreviation of *turn rule.*

Trim. To reduce a story carefully.

Truck. See *turtle.*

Trunk. The main wire of a wire service.

TTS. The abbreviation for *teletypesetter.*

Turn column. A few papers continue column eight, page one, to column one, page two, and eliminate a *jump head.*

Turn rule. A direction to the printer to turn over a *slug* because an addition, *insert,* or correction will be made at that point. The slug then becomes a reminder, which must be removed before printing.

Turtle. A metal cart, often called a truck, used to transport page *forms* to the *mat roller;* often used as a *stone.*

Type high. Any material high enough to print. The standard height of type is .918 of an inch.

Typo. Short for typographical error.

Undated story. A story with no specific geographical focus, such as a war in the Near East, and therefore no specific dateline. The source of the story is printed at the top, such as "United Press International."

Under-dash material. Prepared stories, principally *obituaries,* ready for publication. When an event makes the story timely, first come a few paragraphs about the event, then a *jim dash* or *dinky dash,* and then the prepared material (under, or following, a dash).

Underline. See *cutline;* also *caption.*

Universal desk. A desk that handles copy from several departments of the paper, usually city, wire, and state.

Upper case. See *caps.*

Upstyle. A style that capitalizes more words than most papers do; also called magazine style. Contrast *downstyle.*

Urgent. A wire service designation for an important story, but less important than a *bulletin.*

WF. The *proofreader*'s mark for *wrong font.*

White space. The blank space, also called air, around heads, ad copy, and stories; left blank to make the printed material stand out.

Widow. A one- or two-word line at the end of a paragraph; usually unsightly if the last line of *cutlines* or the first line in a column. See also *bad break.*

Wild. Copy that may run on nearly any inside page. See also *run of paper.*

Wire editor. See *telegraph editor.*

Wirephoto. A system owned by Associated Press for transmitting pictures over wire.

Wrap. To place type in two or more columns under a multi-column headline. See also *break.*

Wrapped up. See *all in hand.*

Wrong font. The designation for a letter of type different from the style used in the story.

Xerography. A new process for printing with static electricity and without ink.

Yellow journalism. Sensational and often deliberately inaccurate reporting.

Editing Exercises

Gene Gilmore
University of Illinois

The Glendessary Press · Berkeley

© 1974 by The Glendessary Press, Inc.
2512 Grove Street, Berkeley, California

Printed in the United States of America.

ISBN 0-87709-223-0

Preface

The stories in this workbook section are filled with mistakes. There are misspellings, grammatical errors, mispunctuations, wrong names, clumsy sentences, errors of fact, verbosities, libelous statements, and even miscorrections. It is difficult to spot them all, for we have laid many traps and snares.

The student's best approach is to read the stories two or three times, as he probably will find errors with each reading. The editor must constantly ask, "Can this be right?" Otherwise, he will glide over the copy making neat paragraph marks and correcting an occasional misspelled word, but letting the subtlest and most misleading errors get by.

After editing a few stories the student is usually ready to try writing headlines along with correcting errors. We provide a headline schedule and the basic directions for a size and "count" that would be appropriate.

Because the work is hard or because some students have a natural impatience, there may be a tendency to race through the drills. To resist the temptation, a student should edit until his attention flags, then take a break, returning to the task when it challenges rather than frustrates him.

In many ways, this is how the work is done on a newspaper copy desk. There is a flurry of copy for an hour or more, then there is a chance for a breather. Copyediting is a skill that requires pacing. Students who pace themselves through the stories in this workbook should be able to do beginning copydesk work reasonably well and do it at least with satisfaction if not with downright pleasure.

Style Book

Copyeditors on a newspaper use a style book to assure consistency in capitalization, abbreviation, punctuation, and similar conventional aspects of print. The following set of rules, very similar to those used by Associated Press and United Press International, forms a style book for the exercises in *Editing in Brief.*

Capitals

Use capital letters sparingly.

CAPITALIZE:

1. All proper nouns, including months, days of the week and seasons.

2. The *Bible,* names of religious denominations and nouns and pronouns referring to the Deity.

3. Names of all races and nationalities, as *Negro, Caucasian, Russian.* But *black* and *white.*

4. Names of all political parties, as *Republican, Socialist, Communist.* But do not capitalize "party."

5. Distinguishing names and nicknames for states, cities, and sections of cities, as *Empire State, the Illini, the East Side.*

6. Names of holidays, as *Veterans Day; Fourth of July.*

7. Titles when they precede a proper noun, as *Gov. Abner Peterson, Sen. Harry Adams, Principal Henry B. Smith;* but *Henry B. Smith, principal.*

8. All parts of an organization's name, as *Ladies' Aid Society, Manufacturers' Association, Bradley University, Central High School, Methodist Church, First Bank, Bank of America.*

9. *pecially coined proper names, as *Typhoon Tillie, Founder's Oak, M. onlight Madness.*

10. Part. of geographical and historical names, as *Atlantic Ocean, Battle of the Bulge, Lake Michigan, Bay of Fundy.*

11. All parts of addresses and conjunctive names, as *Mattis Boulevard, Main Street, Yates Hotel, Gem Theater, Second Ward.*

12. Events and periods of historical note, as *the Declaration of Independence, the Reformation, the American Revolution.*

13. Schools and colleges of a university, but not departments, as *School of Journalism, Liberal Arts College,* but *department of chemistry.*

14. Sections of the country, but not points of the compass, as *the East, the Middle West,* but *east, southwest.*

15. Nicknames of athletic clubs and teams, as *Hawks, Red Sox.*

16. Principal words in the titles of books, plays, lectures and pictures. A beginning article is always capitalized, as *"The Editor and His People."*

17. Abbreviations of college degrees, as *B.A., M.A., LL.D., Ph.D.*

18. Adjectives derived from proper names, as *Chinese student, English grammar.*

19. President, when referring to a specific president of the United States, as *"the President decided,"* but *"a candidate for president";* head of any nation, as *Premier, King, Pope, Queen, Prime Minister.*

20. Positions of authority when used as titles, as *Referee Gibbs, Secretary Talbott,* but *Ron Gibbs, referee.*

21. *Senate, House, Legislature, City Council, Board of Supervisors, General Assembly, Champaign County Circuit Court,* congressional committees.

22. Official names of federal, state or local departments, as *Department of Sanitation, Housing Authority.*

23. Trade and trade marked names, as *Peace rose, Thunderjet, Drano.*

24. Proper names of animals, as *Brown Swiss, Collie, Rhode Island Red.*

25. Fraternal organizations and unions, as *Fraternal Organization of Eagles, International Association of Machinists.*

26. The first word of a direct quotation when the quoted matter makes a complete sentence, as *"Franklin said, 'A penny saved is a penny earned.'"* And *"The problem is this: 'Shall we go or shall we not?'"*

27. Most abbreviations. Some exceptions: *c. o. d.; f. o. b.; m. p. h.; a.m.; p.m.*

28. Foreign names as used by the person. Generally, foreign particles *d', da, della, de* and *von* are lower case.

29. Military decorations, as *Congressional Medal of Honor, Bronze Star, Croix de Guerre.*

Numbers

USE:

30. Numerals for figures 10 and above; words for figures nine and below. Exceptions: numerals for any age, speed, distance, score, height, vote, ratio, date, temperature, dimension, and highway. Always spell out a number starting a sentence, as *Thirty-two students* . . . .

31. Ordinals for political, military, and judicial groups: *4th U. S. Circuit Court of Appeals; 1st Army; 6th Fleet.*

32. Roman numerals for certain names: *Pope Paul V, Peter Adams III, Act IV, World War II.*

33. Words for descriptive numbers: the *Thirties;* he's *a thousand* years old; the *Gay Nineties.*

34. Round numbers above a million, rounding fractions to the second decimal place: *6.75 million, 23 million.*

35. Spell out *cents,* as *15 cents.*

36. Figures for commonly used fractions with whole numbers: *6½, 7¾.* But without whole numbers, use words only: *one-half, three-quarters.*

37. In metric measurements, the decimal: *6.45 meters.*

Punctuation

THE COMMA

38. Punctuates four or more figures except in street numbers, license numbers, etc., as *$5,000; 1272 Salina Street; License 456789.*

39. Does *not* precede "and" and "or" in a series of words, *cotton, wool and silk.*

40. Separates words or figures that might be misunderstood, as *'e said to him, Adams, that. . . .*

41. Separates two rather distinct subjects in a compound sentence, as *The deer are plentiful in the woods, and the fish are numerous in the lakes.*

42. Sets off phrases, clauses, scores, and parenthetic words, as *T ? horse, he said, can't run;* or *Illinois 44, Northwestern 43.*

43. Flanks political designations, as *Sen. Hubert Humphrey, D–Minn., rose to speak.*

THE SEMICOLON

44. Rarely used in newspapers except to divide names and titles, as *John Smith, Peoria; William Jones, Rockford.*

THE APOSTROPHE

45. Used with possessives and in some abbreviations. Generally, words ending in "s" or an "s" sound require only an apostrophe to denote the possessive, as *Jones', Rogers' Rabinowitz', GI's, GIs'* (not possessive), *class of '47.*

46. Makes the plurals of letters but not figures, as *two A's* and *his 3s* (but *OKs).*

THE COLON

47. Follows a statement introducing a direct quotation of one or more paragraphs and after "as follows:"–as *"He gave the following information:"*

48. Denotes fractional clock time, as in track meets: *3:43:02.4 (three hours, 43 minutes, 2.4 seconds.)*

49. Denotes Biblical chapters and verses, as *Matt. 1:14.*

THE EXCLAMATION POINT

50. Seldom used in newspaper writing except in quotations to express surprise or emotion, as *"My God!"*

PARENTHESES

51. Set off material which is not part of the main statement or as an identification, as *Sen. Douglas (D–Ill.)* and *John (Ren) Smith* and *(Editor's Note: We agree.)*

52. Set off figures and numbers in a series, as *"The three reasons are (a) he is not truthful, (b) he has no character and (c) he is a heavy drinker.*

53. Used at the end of a sentence, come before the period, as *The deadline is Feb. 1 (Monday).* A complete sentence in parentheses has the period within, as *(The deadline was Monday.)*

54. When parenthetical matter makes more than one paragraph start each paragraph with a parentheses. Quotation marks on quoted material are placed the same way.

Abbreviations:

ABBREVIATE:

55. Street, Avenue, Boulevard, Terrace in addresses but not in general reference, as *422 E. 14th St.; the house is on Main Street.* But spell out Road, Lane, Oval, Place, Plaza, Port, Circle.

56. Most organizations only after first full reference, as *He was sent to the headquarters for the North Atlantic Treaty Organization, and he was with NATO for 10 years.* FBI, TVA, YMCA, YWCA, AFL-CIO are always abbreviated.

57. Time zones, ships, military terms, as *PDT, AWOL, USS New Jersey.*

58. States which follow cities and villages, as *Walla, Walla, Wash.; Bad Axe, Mich.* But, *He lives in Oklahoma.* Here are the accepted abbreviations:

Ala.	Ill.	Miss.	N.M.	Tenn.
Ariz.	Ind.	Mo.	N.Y.	Tex.
Ark.	Kan.	Mont.	Okla.	Vt.
Calif.	Ky.	Neb.	Ore.	Va.
Colo.	La.	Nev.	Pa.	Wash.
Conn.	Md.	N.C.	R.I.	Wis.
Del.	Mass.	N.D.	S.C.	W. Va.
Fla.	Mich.	N.H.	S.D.	Wyo.
Ga.	Minn.	N.J.		

Do not abbreviate Alaska, Hawaii, Idaho, Iowa, Ohio, Maine or Utah. (As a rule of thumb, abbreviate no state with six letters or less except Texas.)

59. Titles *before* names: *Gov., Gen., Atty., Prof., Supt.* Titles are spelled out and lower case after names, as *Harold Smith, professor of history.*

60. Use *Mr.* only with Mrs., a clerical title or for the dead, as *Mr. and Mrs. Jones; the Rev. Mr. Jones; Mr. Jones, who died in 1967.* Call a woman Miss or Mrs. according to her marital status—or Ms. if she prefers.

61. Number before figures, as *No. 4.*

62. Saint or Sainte in proper names, as *St., Paul, Ste. Marie.*

63. Fort or Mount when used with geographical or military points, as

Mt. Everest, Ft. Douglas; but *Mount Vernon, Fort My*

64. Et cetera to *etc.*

65. Incorporated, Limited, Company when parts of name s *Time, Inc.,; Whelan Ltd.;* the *White Co.*

66. Names of months when used with date, as *Sept. 7, 19* ; but *September 1973.* Spell out March, April, May, June and July. Never abbreviate a day of the week.

67. Only if necessary, per cent in headlines, as *pct.*

68. United States, Union of Socialist Soviet Republics, United Natio. as *U. S., U. S. S. R.,* and *U. N.*

69. Military titles as follows:

Air Force and Army:

General	*Gen.*
Lieutenant General	*Lt. Gen.*
Major General	*Maj. Gen.*
Brigadier General	*Brig. Gen.*
Colonel	*Col.*
Lieutenant Colonel	*Lt. Col.*
Major	*Maj.*
Captain	*Capt.*
First Lieutenant	*1st Lt.*
Second Lieutenant	*2nd Lt.*

Navy:

Admiral	*Adm.*
Fleet Admiral	*Fleet Adm.*
Vice Admiral	*Vice Adm.*
Rear Admiral	*Rear Adm.*
Captain	*Capt.*
Commander	*Cmdr.*
Lieutenant Commander	*Lt. Cmdr.*
Lieutenant	*Lt.*
Lieutenant (jr. grade)	*Lt. (j. g.)*
Ensign	*Ens.*

In the Navy, Chief Petty Officer when used before name is capitalized, but not after. The abbreviation is *C.P.O.* Other Navy ratings would not be understood if abbreviated.

The Army no longer uses the term "technical sergeant."

Enlisted men's abbreviations:

Master Sergeant	*M. Sgt.*
Sergeant, First Class	*Sgt. 1. C.*
First Sergeant	*1st Sgt.*
Sergeant	*Sgt.*
Corporal	*Cpl.*
Private, first class	*Pfc.*
Private	*Pvt.*

Religious Terms and Titles

70. The National Council of Churches of Christ in the United States may be reduced to *National Council of Churches* and referred to later as *the council.*

71. Roman Catholic: *the Rev. Peter Jones, Father Jones* (but never *Mr.*); *The Most Rev. Peter Jones, bishop of the Chicago diocese; Bishop Jones; Francis Cardinal Spellman, archbishop of the New York archdiocese; Cardinal Spellman.*

72. Jewish: *Rabbi Milton Cohen, Rabbi Cohen, Dr. Cohen* (where degree is held). Proper spelling for Jewish holidays is in the dictionary.

73. Christian Science: *Practitioner, Lecturer, Reader* (but never *Rev.* in any form). *Reader Peter Jones of the Second Church.*

74. Seventh Day Adventist: *Elder Peter Jones, Elder Jones.*

75. Latter-day Saints: *Pres. Peter Jones, Pres. Jones; Elder Peter Jones, Elder Jones; Presiding Bishop Peter Jones, Bishop Jones; Bishop Peter Jones of the Presiding Bishopric, Bishop Jones.* The Church of Jesus Christ of Latter-day Saints is not correctly called the Mormon church but its members may be called *Mormons.*

76. Episcopal: A deacon or priest is referred to as *the Rev. Peter Jones* and *the Rev. Mr. Jones.* A dean is *the Very Rev. Peter Jones, the Rev. Mr. Jones, Dean Jones.* An archbishop is *the most Rev. John Jones, the Rev. Mr. Jones, Archbishop Jones.*

77. Lutheran: *Pastor Peter Jones, Pastor Jones; the Rev. Mr. Jones.*

78. All other Protestant denominations give their clergyman the title of *the Rev.,* as in *the Rev. John Jones.* With the last name only, *the Rev. Mr. Jones.*

79. Church terms: *The Rosary* is recited or said, never read. *Mass* is celebrated, said or read. *Benediction of the Blessed Sacrament* is neither held or given; services close with it.

Editing Exercises I

In the following illustration the beginning editor can see how essential it is to improve sentence structure and to watch for errors of fact as well as for the simpler mistakes of spelling, punctuation, and style. Before starting the work, Appendix A should be studied with care.

~~The late~~ President Lyndon B̸.:
Johnson, who died in 1973, left a
legacy of achievement for the civil
rights movement, the Rev. Jess~~i~~e
Jackson told the ~~u~~rban League's
annual meeting today.

⌐Although more should have been
done, the Chicago civil rights leader
added, several key bil̷s were passed
during Johnson's ~~four~~ five years as
'̷resident.

'Johnson appointed the first
bla̷k to the Supreme Court and ~~made~~
~~more~~ ~~ny~~ ~~appointments~~ ~~of~~ ∧blacks to
named more
top job̷ than any president before
or since, ~~Jackson added~~. he said ✗

Flaws: Johnson's middle initial was B. "The late" and "died" are redundant.

Jessie is the feminine spelling. Jackson is male and spells his name Jesse.

Johnson was president for more than five years.

style error

sentence structure ragged.

revision to avoid style error, repetition.

Starters: Sentences

Edit the following sentences, being watchful in particular for redundancies.

1. The man was hung before the sherrif could get to the scene.

2. He could not tell whether or not the man had died from drowning.

3. The money was distributed between Oregon, Wisconsin, and New Hampshire.

4. The body will be interned in Greenlawn Cemetary.

5. Haym Cohen, a Jewish rabbi, will officiate at services.

6. Matilda Wallingford, widow of the latey Judge Arthur Wallingford, won the prize.

7. She blushed a livid red.

8. Her hat, a beautiful orange, came from Bloomingdale's.

9. A conference was held between he and the secretary.

10. Senator William Proxmire, (R-Wis) is the present incumbent.

11. One of the players said the other team played dirty.

12. He said that at this point in time ~~there~~ their is no need for

    those type of programs.

13. Despite all the excitement around them the rescue workers

    remained cool as cucumbers.

14. The committee discussed the subject of sanitation.

15. His wife pre-deceased him by 5 years.

16. The consensus of opinion was that he broadcasted too much

    on the subject.

17. Asked what he thought about the brutal beating he said

    that he was horrified.

18. The ladies said they had less dollars to spend this year.

19. Peter McLaughling got a majority of the votes with 43 per

    cent. Roger Odie got 30 per cent and William Riis got the

    remainder.

20. All of the prople in the accident suffered serious lacerations

    and contusions and are critical in the hospital.

21. The honorable Schuyler Pettibone, regent of the university,

    is currently playing ~~plon~~ Polonious in a Little Theater production

    of Hamlet.

22. He said that in the forseeable future there would be

    be no chance to orientate the students.

23. The reason why he voted for her is obscure.

24. He said that taxwise the budget was sound.

25. Unaware of the fact that Eisler had died, he wondered why
the flag was at half mast on the post office.

26. Rosemary Davis, the president of the bank, said she felt
badly about charging so much interest.

27. Neither John or Sally could walk any further.

8. He is laying down on the job, just like I thought.

29 He bought some stationary so he could write to his friend
in the penitentiery in the Phillipines.

30. They dove into the water as soon as they heard the sudden
explosion.

Starters: Story Segments I

Edit the following story segments, watching in particular for misspellings and typographical errors.

1. Energy conservation effforts by Amercans during December
resulted in electricity and natural gas savings of more than
10 per cent, survey has shown.

2. George C. Calhoun has been swore in as District Attorny.
He becomes the 45th person to take the office. In the 164
years the office has exissted only men have held the position.
Calhoun defeated Mildred Sisal in the general election.

3. Bernard V. Zeeney, 24, was releesed from jail yesterday

when he was able to post $1,500 bale. He has been in jail

for six days on a charge of embezlement.

4.   The Water Conservation Ditsrict will establish a $15 fee

to examine an acer of land for soil ~~cakilty~~. A fee of $25 will

capabilty(i)

be charged to check 10 acers.

5.   A workshop has been set for December 5 to examine econmic

development of the city. Representives of the Chamber of

Commerce, the local universitys urban planing deparment, and a

Harvard economist wll speak. Mayer ~~Hirman~~ Gentry said the work-

Hiram

shop should be ~~helfal~~ because "its time we figured out ways to

helpfal

enlarge the tax bass."

6.   The Munich Haus restaurat was closed mysteriusly yesterday.

Although no announcement has been made customers found the foor

locked when they showed up for lunch. A small "closed" sign was

on the door. Efforts to reach Heinz Roethlisberger, the owner,

have failed.

7.   Charlie McCord scorred 42 points are the Swampstown Mudcats

defeeted the Eagletown Birds last nihgt, 65-64. McCord hit 68

percent of his shotts from the floor to make 15 field goles.

He got the other twelve on free threes.

8.   A zoolagist says a fish pond owner could put trout and

ordinary lake fish into one tank. Al he would have to do, the

sceintist said, would be to pumpliquid oxygen into the depths

so the trout gets air and cool temperature.

9.   Vactioners should plan for trips within 50 m   es of home
this sumer to conserve fuel, Governor Dan Hildwei   annonced
today.   "Many of us have simply put off inspectin   the cities
nearby, he said. New, since there isn't gasline   ogh for long
trips we can see those places we thought we would   ee 'some
time.'" he added.

10.   Taxpayers with relatively simple forms to fi   . should send
them to there nearest International Revenue Servi   e offfice, a
tax expert said today. The IRS will fill out the   forms at no
charge, he addded.

Starters: Story Segments II

Edit the following story segments and stories, watching for misspellin s, name and
punctuation errors, grammatical and typographical mistakes, and style   rrors.

1.   George L. Vann, Assistant Attorney General,   aid the
appeel will cost $5000 dollars.

2.   Benjamin Norris, 39, of 903 N. Shirley Stree , was arrested
about 8 p. m.   He was charged with not having a f rarm owner's
identification card, unnlawful possesion of the w ppon, resis-
ting arrest and agravated assault.

3.   Farmers should be aware of corn leaf affids, which may
strike about mid July especially if the weather is dry he said.

4.   "What I want to know, said the tall middle aged man, "is
why the'll pay the Arrabs $17.00 and me only $3.80?"

5.   The Church seeks rezoning of property they own at 402-404

East Main St. The property now is zoned currently as multiple
family residential. The Church wants the land put into a
central commercial classifcation. It is hoped the new classifi-
cation would assist sale of the proprty.

6. The mayor said the certificates would rdaw intrest at 6 and
one quarter per cent a year. "This will bring us $5400 in revenuew
by next March he avverred."

7. Chicago (AP)-Vincent Starrett, veteran Chicago newsman, who
was considered one of the worlds formost authorities on the
legendary slueth Shylock Holms, is deceased at age 87 years.

8. The 3-year agreement replaces a privately negotiated
agreement which has been in force after relations were normal-
ized in September 1972.

9. A spokesman said a court arguement about eh low bid on
supplying the lisence plates caused the delay. Howlett adver-
tised for bids to manafacture the plates. A firm in Conway,
Arkansas was the low bidder. But Howlette wanted the bid to
be given to a firm in Illinois. The Arkansaw firm went to
court and won.

10. The IBI began November 1 a statewide investgation of
possibble ilegal sales of surplus federal proprty. This was
done after almlst 400,000 dollars in surplus item--mostly trucks
and tools, was disscovered on land owned by a private lake County
contracter.

11. Siro T. Agnue, former vice president, will pay golf with Frank Sinatra at the Pebble Beech Country Club.

12. HMO--Health Maintainence Organization--traces its roots to a clinic in Elk City, Oklahoma during the thirites depression. The concep reeched its' first big scale system in the West Cpast developm3nt of the Kaisar foundation health plan.

Starters: Stories

Be alert for any error or misleading phrases in the following stories.

1.

crash

TANGIER, MORROCCO (AP)-All 105 persons abord a Belgium jet-liner chartered for the Christmas holiday rush were killed when the plane crashed into a mountan in northern Morocco, police said Sunday.

Officials said most of the victims of the terrible crash which occured during a glinding rainstorm Saturday night, were Brench, Belgian, or Morroccan, and included many children. There were 99 passengers and six crew members on the jetliner.

2.

money

A young hotel main has been awarded $10,000 she found in
an Austin Texas hotel room whe was clensing.

Police said they could not find anyone to claim the money
so a judge awareded the sum to Mrs. Esmerelda Janson, 19 years
old.

3.

revenue

The Tuckahoe County Board voted 24 to three yesterday to
put all of it's revenue sharing money from the federal goverment into the general fund.

The three disenters said that the move will allow a tax
cut this year but will laeve the county with a decifit a year
from now.

The County has recieved 1,100,000 dollars in revenue
sharing.

4.

quake

An earth quakey, a rarity in this part of the country,
rolled across the state this morning, causing a lot of fright
but almost no damage.

Houses seemed to itp for a few minutes, a dish here and

and

there fell off tables, cars trembled as though they were falling
apart.

Milton Harbison
A seismologist at Oliver College said the quake was only
able to shake his earthwuake measuring devices. "I'm sure it
scared a lot of people. I even wondered what was oming off.
I've never been present during an earthquake before "

5.

crash

A single engine airplane crashed in the middle of La. e
Airport today, causing a 30-minute delay in the use of the
main airstrip.

The pilot and only occupant of the plane, Doris Wheeler,
was unhurt. She admitted that she landed too fast and the
plane tipped over onto its' noise.

Wheeler said she may have saved her life becuase she
was wearing her motorcycle crash helmet. "I always wear it
when I land", she said.

Miss Wheeler, 27, runs a bridle store in the Easwood
shopping center.

6.

eso

Trevor Murdoch was eledted president of the East Side Organization, a group formed to improve streets, sidewalks traffic movement, and plantings in their part of town.

The election was held last night in the Clarke school.

The group also decided to petition city council for bikeways through the east side. The bikeways would connect with the downtown area and major schools, the organization requests.

Murdoch succeeds George Carmichael, who has been president since the Organization was established two years ago.

7.

calabrese obit

Luigi Calabrese, operate of a cigarette vending business for 35 years, died yesterday at the age of 69 in Mother Cabrini hospital. He had resided for 43 years at 228 North 12th Strcet.

He was born in Brooklyn, New York and moved her 43 years ago with his bride, the former Rose Mariano. SHe and three sons, Frank, Thomas and Juigi, jr., survive.

A Mass of the Resurrection will be held at 10 A. M. Saturday at St. Donato's RC church. Interment will be in meadow Hill Cemetary.

Headline Schedule

For the rest of the drills, students should write headlines as assigned, using the following headline schedule.

A common code on newspapers identifies headline size by numbers. For example, 4/60/2 means that the headline should be four columns of 60-point type, set in two lines. It would look like this:

Weaver gets housing job
as mayor shakes up staff

Note that this is a "downstyle" headline. Except for the first word and for proper nouns, every letter is lower case. Many newspapers have an "upstyle" system, in which all words are capitalized or all words are "up" except prepositions.

The "count" of the headlines used here can be determined by multip ing the count per column by the number of columns the headline will cover. I he previous example, the headline schedule shows that 60 point gets 5½ char ters per column. In 36 point the count is 11 per column. A 2/36/2 would have 2   es, with each line no more than 22. The minimum count could be 19. Remember at type is not flexible. If the count is 22, the headline writer cannot squeeze in 22 .

The single column heads listed at the right of the schedule always wi   ook like the illustrations. A "28" always will have three lines, for example, and t refore it is unnecessary to say "28/3."

When there are roman and italic type faces in the same point size, as t ere are in 42 point, the letter "I" will indicate italic. So the assigned head may b   3/42/2 I. Unless the "I" appears after the numbers, the head is set in roman.

Count headline characters this way:
Lower case *l, i, f, t (lift)* count one-half.*
Punctuation counts one-half. So does the number 1.
Lower case *m* and *w* count 1½.
All other lower case letters and figures count one.
Upper case *M* and *W* count two.
Upper case *I* counts one-half.
All other upper case letters count 1½.
If all letters are capitals, count each as one, except *M* and *W*, which are 1½, and *I,* which is one-half.

* *J* also counts one-half in some type faces.

90 point; count 3½ per column width

Uruguay

(#43)

August housing starts up

8 maximum
42 point

72 point; count 5 per column

Sears spring

(#34)

Moon predates genesis rock, scientists find

14 maximum
34 point

60 point italics; count 5½ per column

Weaver named

(#28)

Columnist calls credibility gaps 'healthy tensions'

16 maximum
28 point

48 point italics; count 7 per column

Fired, he gets bett

Bridge   (#K30)   Kicker:
18 pt. ital under-
lined (15 max.)

It takes two to rob a hand

14 maximum
30 point

42 point; count 8 per column

County sues 4 firms

(#19 freak)

August ore shipments dip

14 maximum
18 point

42 point italics; count 7½ per column

Admits 200 Chicago

(#15 folo)

AHS sees gains for third quarter

18 maximum
14 point

24 point italics; count 12 per column

Back tougher penalties for killing of eagles

(#12)

24 maximum
12 point

Dutch Starfighter falls
THE HAGUE (UPI) — A
Dutch air force Starfighter

Heads to Write

The following "orders" based on our headline schedule can be used for writing headlines to the stories in the next section.

Story	Instruction	Slug	Story	Instruction	Slug
1--2/36/2 (filter)			19--2/24/1 (with budget)		
2--3/36/1 (author)			20--28 (annex)		
3--28 (coach)			21--28 (drug)		
4--2/42/2 (cadre)			22--12 (Rhode)		
5--3/48/2 (snow)			23--3/48/2 (airport)		
6--19 (soy)			24--K30 (brace)		
7--28 (Kennedy)			25--2/42/2 I (blaze)		
8--2/24/2 (noise)			26--2/36/1 (bridge)		
9--15 (marriage)			27--34 (baseball)		
10--19 (drunk)			28--2/42/2 (lawsuit)		
11--19 (bridge)			29--3/48/2 (park)		
12--2/42/2 (Harrison)			30--28 (race)		
13--19 (aging)			31--2/24/2 (wedding)		
14--19 (chorus)			32--34 (gas)		
15--2/36/2 (paper)			33--2/36/2 (axident)		
16--3/42/1 (claims)			34--2/42/2 I (sewer)		
17--2/36/2 (school)			35--19 (litter)		
18--8/72/1 (budget) with 3/48/2 readout			36--2/36/2 (canvas)		
			37--3/48/2 (recruit)		

Story	Instruction	Slug
38	3/36/1	(pain)
39	19	(Neiman)
40	28	(trail)
41	2/42/2	(lottery)
42	34	(cop)
43	4/48/1	(tech)
44	2/24/2	(fish)
45	28	(guerrilla)
46	2/48/2	(rate increase)
47	2/36/2	(Hamlet)
48	3/48/2	(congress)
49	28	(Viet)
50	3/48/2	(hospital)
51	28	(sewage)
52	3/36/3	(steal)
53	2/36/2	(stox)
54	nothing	

Story	Instruction	Slug
55	3/42/1 I	(amnesia)
56	4/48/1	(securities)
57	28	(bomb)
58	nothing	
59	2/42/2	(meningitis)
60	3/36/1	(Brown recluse)
6.	28	(Ag)
62	36/2	(transit)
63	34	(acial)
64	19	(concert)
65	28	(energy
66	19	(Smith)
67	(train)	

Stories 67-70 concern one accident. 5/72/2 on TRAIN. 2/36/2 on MEXEY.

| 71 | 2/42/2 | (sharing) |

Editing Exercises II

Stories for Scrutiny

1.

filter

Filters on storm sewers emptying into Rusty creek were proposed today by Mayor Karl Zeisske before the city council's Environment Committee.

The storm ~~sewes~~ (sewers) he said, carry the water that in effect, washes the streets. This is dirty water, containing oil, paper scraps, plain dirt, and some chemicals.

The result is more pollution to the Creek, he told the Committee. Since the sewer pipes are a few feet above the creek's surface, he said, filters could be easily installed. The water would go through the filters quickly but the impurities, in the main, could be captured.

Zeiske said that the filters could be ~~emptied~~ changed every month or after a particularly heavy storm.

He said the fitlers would cost about eight dollars for a ~~12~~ 24 inch pipe, the largest in the city. The city has 42 such pipes. He estimated the cost at about $1,000 a year.

The Committee voted to look further into the proposal and report within a month to the Council.

2

author

A local author has had her 18th book published within
18 years.

Mrs. Edyth McWittie, the author, said she hopes to keep
writing a book a year until she is a hundred.

"I. t will give me fifty books and it will be time to retire,"
she s id, *with a smile* in her home yesterday.

The latest book is called "Walls and Barricades," a novel
about barr ers erected by old people to keep them from understanding the young.

"I have be n concerned that people cluster into groups
their own age and with their own interests and then become
hostile to other grou s," she said. "Perhaps my next book
will be how young people often scoff at the old and make old
age for many a time of misery."

She really means the next book after the one she is half-
written already. Her current work deals with the history of
the major rivers which empty into the Mississippi. Rivers have
been a keen interest of Mrs. McWittie for thirty years and
three of her books have been on midwestern rivers: the
Illinois, the Fox, and the Missouri.

Her latest book, published by Green & O'Shaugnessy, is on
sale at local bookstores.

3.

coach

Erich Morrow was fired as football coach at Greening High School today. His team has lost their last eleven games.

The School Board said they would set up a committee to look for a new coach. "We want a winner and we don't care how he wins," board president Horace Stuart declared.

Stuart said he thought it would be fair to consider on of the three assistant coaches for the Number One job, "even though they have had a role in the defeats, too."

Morrow has coached at Greening for the last 9 years. He had been a star guard at Oliver College and thejob at Greening was his first coaching assignment.

Morrow said he would quit coaching. "I did fine the first seven years, but then I lost my touch." He said he planned to sell insuranse.

4.

cadre

Mary Banfield, member of Women's Cadre, spoke about the rights of women in the Browning Hotel yesterday.

She said that despite years of efort the schools in the city still are hiring men at a faster rate as teachers than t. y are women. She spoke at the Cadre's fourth annual conven 'on. Banfield is chairman of the Human Rights Committee.

3y now every main business or professional group has its tokt woman", she said, but they still leave us out of the decisi n-making and out of the key jobs.

She rec mmended that delegations from Cadre and other interested gro ps atten school board meetings to protest "the excessive hiring of male teachers." She added, school teaching has been a female preserve--except at the administrative level-- and now their trying to take that away from us."
She said that as soon as Cadre clears up the problem of sex discrimination at the public school level the group will move to an attack on discrimination against women at Oliver College.

"We know that there are only three women on the faculty there," Mrs. Banfield said. "Two of them are instructers and one of them an assistant professor.

"The assistant professor has been there nine years. Both of the others has been there four years each. Almost none of the men even has the lowly instructor rank," she said.

5.

snow

9 inches of snow were dumped onto the city last night,
forcing the city to rent plows to get the snow off the main
streets.

They hadn't made much progress by noon today for Only
three key streets and the downtown area were plowed.

Weather man Jorge Schweikert said another 6 inches will
fall tonight and that the temperature will fall tomorrow to
five degrees.

Mayor Kark Zeisske apologized for the slow removal. "We
just aren't prepared for this kind of storm. As everyone
knows we rarely get more than 4 inches at a time. The seven
rented plows didn't start work until 8 am. this morning. But
all plows will keep running through the night to get the streets
clear. I'm hoping that the weatherman is in error and that we
get no more snow."

Zeisske said that the plows rent for fifty dollars a day. City
highway crewmen operate the plows.

The crews intend to open streets where city busses run.
Only a few buses have been able to operate today and none of
them could make full runs.

Many downtown business places did not open today. Store
clerks could not get to work. It didn't matter much, because
customers couldn't get there either.

6.

soy

A strike at the Zenith Soybean Company e. d today when
the firm agreed to set up a pension plan for tl workers.
Some 250 employees are effected. *The strike sta ted six days ago.*

th in

The indepndent union at the plant settled it↗ wage demands
four days ago, winning a raise of 22 cents an hour.

The pension plan will provide that nay employee ho has
worked a minimum of 20 years with the firm shall recei e, with
Social Security $400 a month at age 65. There had been o
pension plan at Zenith before.

Base pay at the plant now will be $3.27 an hour.

7.

Kennedy

District Attorney Erica C. Kennedy siad today that she
would not seek re-election when her term expires next year.

She said that she has held the job for seven years and
that she wants to return to the practice of law.

Mrs. Kennedy, A Democrat, has been one of the most opopular
vote-getters in the history of the party locally. She got 58
per cent of the vote when she first ran and 69 percent when she
was elected for a second term.

She has been able to get convictions in 93 per cent of the cases brought to trail in the years she has held the job. She prosecuted the major cases herself, leaving her staff of 16 assistants to handle the lesser jobs.

Only one other woman holds such a job in the whole nation.

8.

noise

Take care, motorcyclists, jackhammer operators, and people with loud voices.

The city's noise meter has arrived.

Mayor Karl Zeisske said police will art using the equipment tomorrow to enforce the city's new noise control ordinance.
From time to time The meter will be placed at major traffic intersections to measure the noise made by all kinds of vehicles. If they make too much noise the fine can be $50.

Residents should complain, Zeisske said, if they hear repeated loud noises. Police then will check the sound to see if it violates city law.

Zeisske said that motorcycles suspected to of being too loud will be started and tested. If they fail to meet standards of quiet the owners will have to muffle the machine or risk run the risk of a fine.

9.

marriage

Stuttgart, Germany (UPI)-Would-be marriage suiters should make the search for a partner a do it yourself operation, according to the nation's central consumor organization.

The organizations, in a "Black Book" on West Germany's marriage bureaus, siad it had found hardly any worthy of reccomendations.

10.

drunk

Winslow Hamilton, 32 was convicted of drunk driving in County court today. He was sentenced to 30 days in jail and to a fine of $1,000.

Judge Angus MacKenzie presided.

Hamilton, of 143 Dewitte street, had drivven his new Europea car off 19ncoln avenue into some bushes near the intersection with Bundy drive November 23.

Police arrested him then and contened that a half empty bottle of rye whiskey was found inthe car.

Hamilton, who is a welding instructor at the Central Vocational School, had pleaded not guilty. He was convicted by a six-member jury.

11.

bridge

Two of the lanes on the whitman Street bridge will be
closed for the next four days. The city public works department will resurface the lanes with bituminous concrete. The
bridge has four lanes.

The other two lanes were surfaced with the blacktop
material two weeks ago.

Police Chief J. Howard Spaatz advised motorists to avoid
a jam on the bridge by shifting to the Whittier Street bridge
six blocks to the south.

12.

Harrison

The president of the Teacher's Union at Olima University
will not have his contract renewed because he as been denied
tenure and a promotion.

The case involves Roger B. Harrison, assistant professor
of history, who was highly recommeneded by his colleges for
promotion. Such promotion automatically would have given him
tenure.

Harrison has been on the faculty for six years. He is
31. The university has an "up or out after six" policy,
although it is not always enforced. This means that an
assistant professor must be promoted after six years on the
faculty or he will be dismissed.

Chancellor Paul C. Endicott said he would not comment on the case beacuse Harrison is appealing the rejection of promotion.

Harrison would not say anything either for the same reason.

Several members of the history faculty, however, said ina statement that the refusal to promote Harrison "is clearly a move to penalize him for his attempt to unionize the members of the faculty. This is a violation of federal law and we intend to fight for his vindication."

Horace B. Witherspoon, chairman of the history department, said he was "bitterly disappointed" that Harrison had not been promoted. "I have him the highest recommendation," he said.

Five of harrison's student are circulating a petition in Harrison's behalf. The petition contends that Harrison was in the top 10 per cent of the teachers they had had in their years on campus. They said that in a half day of effort they had 32 signatures. Harrison teaches three classes and has a total of 74 sutdents.

The appeals procedure on promotion is complicated. The appellant sends a letter to the appeals board and asks for a rehearing. The appellant may appear in person. The board is made up of the chairman of the original promotion committee, Ira McGraw, Vice Chancellor Homer B. Evans, and Charles F. Attlas, a professor biology.

If Harrison fails there he will be able to go to court.

13.

aging

The governor's regional adviserycommittee on the aging
will open a conference that will last for three days$\wedge$at the
                                                    today
Abbott Conference Center.

The committee, with 15 members, will consider the needs
of the elderly in Tillingham County and the four counties
which surround it.

Among reports to be presented will be ones on hospital
care, health care, transportation difficulties, recreation,
and nutrition.

Mayor Karl Zeisske will welcome the committee and escort
the 15 members on a tour of four senior citizen centers in the
community.

14.

chorus

"Spirit of the Mind", a black chorus from Northern
Illinois University will perform in a free concert Sunday in
Rockham auditorium. The time will be 3 p. m.

The chorus, which has 75 members, will sing a variety of
afro-American songs. An organizt, trumpeter and pianist will
accomany the singers. The director is Herschel Emory, a
member of the music faculty at NIU.

The performance is sponsored by the Afro-American Culture
Center, 114 North Goodwin St.

15.

paper

Four state government departments will use recyceled

paper from now on, David D. Mandel, executive assistant to

Governor Charles B. Elliott, said today in an interview.

The departments are public health, education, environmental

labor

rotection, and public instruction.

Each will finish their supply of paper on hand and then

buy on'y recycleled material, he said. Mandel said the change

will be s'ightly more expensive for a few months and then the

cost would b> about the same.

"We think the eventual cost will be much lower." he said,

"For we simply will not be consuming basic resources. Trees,

for example, are going to get more expensive if we keep chop-

ping them up into paprr."

economy

"The health of our state depends on our ability to use and

reuse existing resources instead of using the materials once and

then paying to bury them in landfills. The governor is 100 per

cent behind this program."

16.

claims

A person who fells that he has been cheated can go to
court for a $9.50 fee and be his own lawyer.

All he has to do is go to the court house and find the
probate court division. He fills out papers accusing a person
                          He pays a $9.50 fee.
or company of unjestix treatment. ∧ The charge may be failure
fulfill a warranty,
∧to meet an agreement, the sale of shoddy merchandise, or
refusal to pay a bill.

A cleark will mail a copy of the charges to the accused
by certifyed mail. A̶x̶k̶x̶r̶x̶i̶x̶x̶d̶x̶k̶x̶x̶i̶x̶x̶x̶x̶k̶x̶ A notice of a trial
date is included.

On trial day the person bringing the charges can tell
                                  e
the judge his story. The defendₐnt can tell his side. The
judge rules for the plaintiff he gets his complaint settled and
is reimbursed for court costs. If the judge rules for the
        e
defendₐnt, of course, the plainfiff is out of luck and his $9.50.

Experience in the local courts show that the plaintiffs
win about 90 percent of the cases. There's one main reasons"
the defendant doesn't show up so the judge rules immediately
for the plaintiff.

17.

school
Colorado educators are using the wheel as the basis for
~~edcation~~ educating the childran of Chica*N*go and Indian harvest
workers, the school board was told last night.

James R. Fridley, representing the Colorado Department of
Education, said that vans go to the *major* migrant labor camps with
dual-language materials and teach the children where they live.
"Its' something like the old one-room schoolhouse". he said.
"except that we go to them."

He recommended that the school board run a similar
sim.liar program in the *remote* ~~rural~~ areas of the district, where
there ar several small migrant labor camps in the summer.
James said that the vans would not have to limit education to
children xxdx for many adults would profit from the materials
and instruction too.

The board decided to consider the proposal and make a
decision at the meeting next month.

The materials are both in English and Spanish, since so
many of the migrants are either Mexican or Mexican-Americans.

Fridley said that he thought it was important that all
                    English
children learn to speak ~~Spanish~~ good. He added he would be
pleased if adults did too but he would like adults to learn
enough English so they can make themselves understood in
fundamental conversation in stores and in public offices.

Stories to Tighten

For the following stories the editor should make a special effort to tighten the copy, eliminating or rearranging phrases, sentences, or paragraphs as necessary.

18.

budget

The city council last night approved a 12.6 million dollar budget. The vote was 11-3, with the dissenters claiming that the budget was too small to do the work that needs to be done in the city.

The budget is 15 per cent higher than the current budget, which goes out of business at the end of the fiscal year today.

Most of the increase was in public works where the department plans to buy substantial amount of heavy equipment to improve streets, sewers and landfill operations.

Public works will spend $3.67million. About $300,00 will go to pay for 63 more acres for eventual use as a landful. the land adjoins the present landfill to the north.

The budget calls for expanding the police force by 12 men at an extra cost of $120,000 since rookie policemen in the next fiscall year will get $10,000 a year. No new firemen will be added.

~~May Ka~~ Mayor Karl Zeisske's proposal for a 4.7 per cent salary increase in all departments was approved.

The budget also approves an expenditure of $800,000 for urban renewal. It is the first time in two years that the city has ~~appropriated~~ alocated any money for urban renewal. The

decision means that the city expects to revi ` the program
which faded out after 17 acres were cleared oi the north side.

City council has indicated that it would n approve any
urban renewal project that clears large tracts. rious
councilmen have made clear that they support only z t urban
renewal--that is, removal of only clearly decayed bui lings
and replacing them with sound structures.

While the budget is going up 15 percent there is not
tax increase planned. The budget anticipates heavy increas 3
in sales tax and income tax. In both these cases, the taxes
are collected by the state and xxix part of the take is given
to the cities. The city utility tax is expected to bring an
extra $100,000 on the grounds that next winter may be normal.
The past winter was mild and natural gas consuption was lower,
cutting into utility tax revenue.

The three dissenting councilmen on the budget were James
Fischer, Amanda Whitcomb, and Charles B. McLean.

Mrs. Whitcomb, saying she spoke for the three, said that
the budget calls for no increase except in salaries for the
part department.

"We have a opportunity to buy three small tracts that
would make excellent little parks," she said, and it is a
shame that the budget does not call for enough to buy even
one of them."

"The tracts are in the north end where there are only two parks. We need some parks within easy walking distance of many people and where small children may go by themselves," she said.

"The city has not increased its park acreage in seven years, despite the fact that the city population has grown 14% in that time. Therefore, we are going to vote against the whole budget."

Zeiske said that the acreage has not increased but that the parks have been improved in that time.

19

with budget

This a digest of the city budget past last night by City Council:

Extimated Revenue for coming Fiscal Year:

Property Taxes	$5,684,000
Sales tax	3,200,00
Utility tax	1,630,000
Income tax	1,005,000
Fines and costs	665,500
Building fees	135,000
Licenses	163,400
Investments	54,000
Miscellaneous	23,000
	11,560,900 12,560,900

Requested expenditures

Mayor's Office	137,716
City Council	74,360
Legal Department	83,000
Finance Department	1,227,900
Human Relations Commission	62,450
Planning	143,500
Civil Defense	25.400
Light Dept.	970,650
Urban Renewal	600,000
Police Department	2,450,500
Fire Department	2,200,600
Public Works	3,671,500

Surplus   76,824

12,560,900

20

annex

City Council is expected to annex 155 lots now aurrounded by by the city at its June 19 meeting.

The lots are in the 1800 and 1900 blocks of Anderson St., the 200 and 2100 blocks of Burkwood, the 1700 block of Evergreen Court, the 2400 block of Larch ~~and~~ the 1500 -1800 blocks of Maple, and the 1500-1900 blocks of Pine. ~~street~~

The lots became surrounded by the city limits a month ago when the city council annexxed the Crestwood Shopping Center on Philadelphia (Road). State law says that when a region less than 60 acres in size is surrounded by ~~city~~ land in a city the territory can be annexxed by a simple majority of the City Council.

The City will be able to add about a half million dollars
roles
in assessed valuation to its tax ~~rolls~~ by the Anexation. All of the properties are residential.and most of the homes have a market value of $30,000.

The city utility tax also will be paid by all the 155 householders. The rate is 2 and one-half percent.

The city also will benefit from a greater share of state income tax refunds and a bigger share of state $ gasoline tax rebates. ~~rebates.~~

21.

drug

Hubert C. Stuart, 22, has been sentenced to two to eight years in the penitentary for stealing drugs from two physician's offices.

Circuit Judge Charles C. Levandowiski imposed the sentence yesterday after Stewart ~~pleaded~~ pled guilty to petty theft and to maintaining a dwelling used by drug users.

Martin Champion, 17, wasfound dead of an overdose of drugs in Stuarts' mobile home March 17. Stuart was arrested the next day.

Stuart admitted theift of drugs from the offices of Dr. Homer Anderson and Dr. David Winslow, who have their offices in the Medical Building, 1805 W. Eureka Str-et.

Public Defender Jay W. Burgess represented Stuart and was able to get the burglary charges reduced to petty theft in ex-change for the guilty plea.

22.

Rhode

Salisbury, Rhodesia (AP-"Was the accused concsious or unconsious when you saw him at the clinc" the lawyer asked a witness in court. "He was pretending to be conscious but he wasn't," replied the witness.

23.

airport

A U. S. grant has been approved for a study of the future
of Hamilton Airport. The grant from the Federal Aviation
Agency totals $47,000.

Manager Ralph Petersen of the airport said that it was
likely the Airport Board would spend almost all the amount to
hire a consultant. The remainder of the money would be spent
for administrative details.

Petersen said that the airport must decide how much it
needs to be enlarged and how the airport should be financed.

The airport now is financed locally by the City Council,
which provides $50,000 a year. The state pays $150,000 and
the federal government twice that much. *The rest of the expenses
are met by landing fees, leases to airlines, a restaurant, etc*
Peterson said that some members of the City Council want
to have the county pay some of the cost. They contend, he
reported, that many people outside the city use the airport
but have to pay nothing to support it at the local *level,* ~~live.~~

Meanwhile, a coalition of groups indicated opposition
either to airport expansion or to the financing of the airport.

Willis T. Baggs of the NAACP said that the way the airport is financed is another good example of "welfare for the
rich." "It's not the poor people who use the airport. You
never see a poor man out there, but the state subsidizes it,
the feds subsidize it and the city subsdizes it. Maybe the

wspapers ought to list those people who go to the airport
nd take those 'welfare' flights."

The local Council against Noise (CAN) said that it was
strenously opposed to expanding the airport. Rebecca M.
Harbison, the chairman, said that "already sizable areas of
the city have to endure the roar of the jets 80 times a day.
Bigger runways can be expected to bring bigger roars. Wexhaxe
kax If this is progress then we are against progress."

The airport now has 40 daily flights. Persumably Mrs.
Harbison was counting a landing and takeoff for every flight.
Small planes account for about 200 flights a day from the
airport.

24.

brace

Folsom, California (UPI)-Two Folsom prison inmates, one
an expert at harness making and saddel repair have volunteered
to design and build a totally unique neck brace for an eight
year old boy. The boys doctor called the task "almost impossible".

The boy, Keary Allison, was severely burned in a camping
acident in the Sierra Nevada Mountains west of here last
October. The prisoners, Donald Baxter and Morgan Leach, each
of whom is 52, read a newspaper appeel and volanteered to
produce the brace. The brace will protect the boy's newly
grafted skin.

blaze

A fire destroyed the Fromm shoe store on Main Street last night and for an hour threatened to spread to the whole block.

By using an aerial ladder at close range, Firemen were able to drench the roofs of nearby buildings and avert spreading of flames.

Firemen still had to fight the conflagration for more than five hours before they could get it out. The ruins were still smouldering this morning.

J. Walter Fromm said that nothing could be removed from his store. He estimated his inventory at $120,000 dollars with fixtures worth 30,000 dollars. The building, he said, has a market value of $150,000. He added that he did not know how much of this would be covered by insurance.

No cause of the fire has been determined. But Fire Chief Asher Wilson said there is no reason to suspect arson. "The fire was going to good by the time we got there that there was no chance to look for causes." He said the alarm was given by passerbys who saw the back of the store ablaze.

"Maybe is the weather hadn't been so cold last night more people would have been out and someone would have spotted it earlier," Wilson Said. The temperature was 8 degrees when the fire was reported at 8:15 p.m.

The cold made life miserable for the firemen. Their rubber coats and helments and boots were coated with ice.

Wilson said he tried to get his men into a war area for a few minutes every hour. No one was injured or fros itten, he reported.

A fresh crew of firemen from Fire House No.   in the southeast part of town came on duty at midnight an by 1:30 a.m. all firemen except three, who stood guard, returned o their quarters.

26.

bridge

Money, Miss. (AP-The bridge followed Billy Joe McAl ster into the Tallahatchie River yesterday.

The bridge from which Bill Joe jumped in Bobby Gentry s hit popular song, "Ode to Billy Joe" fell into the river during the night.

Police authorities and other city officials said they did not beleive anyone was on the bridge when it collapsed, but an investigation was launched.

Leflore County Supervisor Ray Tribble had been trying to persuade the highway department ot replace the structure but said he was advised the old bridge was as solid as Gentry's song.

27.

baseball

The Jefferson High School Tigers baseball team shut out
Sc̲h̲weitzer High yesterday 3-2 when pitcher George Brill slammed
a home run with two men aboard.

Brill drove his homer into deep center field with one
out in the 9th inning.

His coach, Dick Walpole, said later, "How's that for
having confidence in your pitcher? I thought of yanking him
for a pitch hitter but then figured he could hit as well as
anyone on the bench."

Until the ninth, the Tigers had had only three dinky
hits off mel Clark, who went all the way for Schweitzer.
But in the last of the ninth, Shortstop Pedro Jiminez drilled
a ball over second base and advanced to second when right
fielder Charlie Adams hit a Texas Leaguer over first. Brill
hit the first pitch for his homer.

Brill had not been particularly effective on the mound.
He allowed 10 hits and four walks and men got on base in every
inning.

Schweitzer scored in the first when First Baseman Roger
McIntosh doubled and Catcher Horace Marshall singled. Another
run was obtaned in the sixth when McIntosh walked, stole second
and came home when Clark hit a long single to right.

28.

lawsuit

A suit for fraud was filed in Tillingham County Court today against the ABC Appliance Emporium by Carlton Huberman, who calls himself the "Ralph Nader of the cornfields."

Huberman's suit ~~contends~~ alledges that ABC consistently refused to meet warrantie requirements on ~~his~~ their products. "Evidence can be presented, the suit contends "that 14 buyers of electric ranges would not get satisfaction when the ranges were able to give heat on only two of the four burners. 11 purchasers of refrigerators will be able to testify that the refrigerators never got colder than 52 degrees. 9 purchasers of power lawn mowers will testify that they mowers almost never could be started. In all caases ABC would not repair or replace the merchandise even though none of the products worked from the day of purchase."

Glenn H. Fenstemacher, owner of ABC, said he would have no comment because he first wanted to consult with legal council.

Huberman is seeking new merchandise for all the equipment he mentions in the suit and $50,000 penalty. He is a lawyer with offices in the Smith Bldg.

29.

Park

The Park District hired John Sommerfield as superintendent last night and approved his plan to landscape the new Martin Luther King Park.

The plan calls for the planting of typical trees and shrubs but also for planting vegetation that once flurished in this area but ~~when~~ which has since become rare or extinct. He said there are at least 20 kinds of plants in the latter catagory.

The park now is a bare 20 acre field in the southeast part of the city.

Somerfield said that he wants to ring the park with a belt of trees, mixing conifers with decidous varieities, so there will be green in the park all year long.

He added that he wants to place trees in shrubs in a way that picnickers will be able to have a little privacy. "By a little organization," he told the commissioners, we can have little picnic areas no bigger than the space taken up by four or five cars. The areas can open into a grassy field."

The plan, which will take three years to complete will cost about $20000, he said. Most of the trees and shrubs are available in the city nursery.

The Park District already has bought playground equipment which will be placed in the east side of the park and has contract for building four tennis courts, two basketball courts, and a softball diamond in the west side.

The land for the park was donated by Mrs. Vivian Shaugnessy, widow of the late Patrick Shaugnessy, a land developer,
who died three years ago. The only stipulations in her gift
was that it be used as a park only and that it be named after
the civil rights leader.

Sommerfield is 24 and a recent graduate of the University
of Wisconsin with a degree in landscape architecture. He has
worked summers for the Park District for the last three summers.
The job of superintendent is a new one. He will assist General
Manager Martin Carmichael and direct the park maintainence crews.

30.

race

United Nations, New York (AP) A report by the UN Special
Committee on Aparthied says South Africa has "continued in the
past year to intensify repressive measures in order to suppress
all resistance" to its policy of seperating the races.

The report yesterday also said the number of people in
prison for violating security laws has dropped more than 15
percent from 549 to 464 in the past year.

The report said South Africa uses "repressive legislation...which violates the cannons of the Rule of Law and empowers
the goverment to detain persons indefinly without trail and to
subject them to arbitrary restrictions."

wedding

Susan Saybrook, daughter of Mr. and Mrs. Quentin Saybrook, 1709 S. Pine Stret, was married Saturday in First Presbyterian church, to Bruce V. Gallagher, son of Mr. and Mrs. V. Schulyer Gallagher of Gross Pointe, Mich.

Some 400 guests attended the ceremony conducted by the Rev. Dr. Ross W. Barnitt.

The bride wore a white knee-length gown of tafetta and a small xx vale of white lace. She carried a bouquet of white and red roses.

Mrs. Robert W. Browne, a college classmate of the bride, was maid of honor. She wore a a pink dress that was cut the same as the bride's.

The best man was Bradshaw Williams of Royal Oak, Michigan. He is a cousin of the bridegroom's.

The ceremony was followed by a reception in the church parlors.

The newlywesd will spend their honeymoon at Niagra Falls and in New England.

The bride is a graduate of Ohio State University and has been employed as a social worker in the public schools here. The bridegroom is an alumni of Bax Brown's University in Providence, Rhode Island. He is a stockbroker in Detroit. The couple will live in Gross Pointe when they return from their honeymoon to Niagra Falls and New England.

32.

gas

Higher gas rates will be paid by some 6,000 suburban residents as a result of a decision yesterday by the State Commerce Commission.

The Zenith Gas Company, which serves the area but not the region inside the city limits, was granted a 6.7 percent (average) increase. The company estimated that the average householder will pay $1.40 more a month, or $17 a year.

Most householders will pay about 5 per cent more and large businesses and industries will pay about 9 per cent more.

The rate increase also will effect some 50,000 people in the three counties to the west. Consolidated Gas supplies gas to residents of the city.

Zenith was upset by the SCC decision. The company had asked for a 9.2 per cent increase in all categories of rates. The commission granted the increase for business but reduced it for householders.

Joseph B. Paine, general manager of Zenith, said the SCC decision "did not grant us the relief we need." Another rate increase cannot, under SCC rules, be sought for a year.

33.

axident

A Hamilton farmer, aged 86, was instantly killed when he drove his car off a side road into the path of a semitrailer south of the village of Hamilton at 11 a. m. today.

The farmer is Albert C. Wheeler, 86, of Route Two, Hamilton. The accident occured two miles from his farm, where he lives alone. Wheelr had no passengers in his car.

Coroner Dwight W. Heath said there would be an inquest, although there seemed to be little doubt but what Wheeler pulled onto U. S. 57 in front of the big truck. The inquest be at 7 p. m. tomorrow in Court Room C. of the Tillingham County Courthouse.

The truck was driven by Elmer Slovonsky, 24, of Chicago. He was driving a truck woned by the Mackay Trucking Company of Racine, Wisc. Slovonsky was not hurt.

Wheeler had no survivors. His wife Marie died four years ago and their son, Albert, jr., was killed on Okinawa during World War Two.

The city of the wreck was where two out-of-state motorists were killed exactly one year ago today.

Wheeler was bonr and raised on the farm. He was never lived in any other place, his neighbors reported to reporters yesterday.

34.

sewer

The treetment of waste will be increasingly expensive
for several communities in the county through 1990.

The water supply is expected to be adequate for the
period except when there would be a sudden demand, such as
at the time of fires.

These predictions were made yesterday in a special report
by the county's Regional Planning Commission. The predictions
are part of a plan which must be accepted by varios state and
federal agencies before the communities can qualify for state
and federal funds for water supplies and sewer disposal.

The communities of Sumner, Buchanan, Forest Hill, and
Tylerville have applied for financial help to construct their
first sanitary sewers and sewage treatment plants. Wastes are
handled by septic tanks in each community now. None of the
towns ~~has~~ *have* more than 1,200 residents. The village of Elm Hall
also plans to apply for help.

The RPC said that other hamlets in the county probably
can get along until 1990 without sanitary sewers because the
places have not grown for 20 years and do not promise to get
bigger.

Federal and state funds may pay up to half the cost of
water supply expansion and up to two-thirds the cost of sewer

lines and sewage treatment plants. The RPC report, however
said that even with the outside aid the cost over the years
for each householder will be several hundred dollars.

In the village of Sumner, for example, it was thought
that laying sewer lines to the 248 homes and business places
and construcing a treatment plant would cost two millon
dollars. Even if state and federal funds paid $1,400,000 the
rest of the cost would be $600,000. This would come to
$2,400 for each home. Bonds would be sold to finance the
construction and the bonds would be retired over 20 years,
the RPC said. Thixx Interest on the bonds would add sub-
santially to the cost, the reprot concluded.

35.

Litter

New York (UPI) Insted of being fined or sent to jail
                                communities
convicted litterers in many U. S. committes are being put to
                          litter
work cleaning up their own littlng and what other people litter.

This is the report filed today by Allen H. Seed, Jr.,
executive x vice president of Keep America Beartiful in observing
that 24,520 persons were arrested for littering in this country
in 1970 the latest year form which statitics are available.

Of the litterbugs convicted, 5,230 were arrested. Fines
paid for littering came to a total of $243,830.

36.

canvas

Students for Gustafson will canvas the city over the weekend in an attempt to lay groundwork for a successful campaign to elect their man to Congress.

"State Senator Charles B. Gustafson deserves to be promoted to congress," Chairman Thomas B. Flusche said, "And we are going to work hard to get him there."

Flusche said that more than 100 students will fan over the city for three days to find where Gustafson's support is. Those who show interest in our candidate will be put on computer lists so we can call them again."

The student work, he said, is being corrdinated with the district campaign workers.

"We know that Gustafson is a man of principal and a man with an outstanding record in the state capitol. While he is particularly attractive to young people we aim in our canvas to find the middle-aged older voters who have been helped so much by the senator's position on the issues."

He noted that Gustafson had pushed through an ordinace which provides for social clubs for the elderly in every community of more than 2,500 persons.

37.

recruit

The recruitment of athletes by our universities demans
those universities by having them trade in what amounts to
a "flesh market," the sports editor of the Denver Star said
in a speach here last night.

"When a university says to a high school boy, 'We want
your dody for four years!' it is the crassest kind of exploitation that leads to every dirty trick that man can advise,"
Jack Temple told the regional conference of the American
Association of University Professors.

"Universities cheapen themselves and display rank
hyprocrisy when they pretend that athletes deserve special
treatment and when they pretend that under-the-table lures
do not fluprish in almost every school."

Temple told the conference at Oliver College that already
schools "openly provide free tuition, room, board, books, and
a $15 a month spending money."

"Some of the worst tales handouts to athletes are not true
but only some of them. It is peculiar that so many top athletes
drive around in new Pontiacs and Buicks when they come from
poor families."

"The kind of exploitation of the athletes is particularly
bad for blacks. Most of them get used for the four years--or
until they are permanently injured--and then tossed out without
a decent education and with no skill except in playing a game.
Only a handful are good enough to turn pro."

"I know of a sophmore at a leading university where the coach arranges for someone else to take all of his exams except in physical education. This is an assistant coach, of course, for the head coach doesn't want to know about such things."

"I know of dozens of other cases where the entrance examinations for athletes are rigged. And I could document at least a hundred cases where an athlete looses his scholarship as soon as he is seriously hurt or as soon as it is clear that he is not varsity caliber.

"Universities have a huge investment in their athletic plants and are reluctant to scrap the high-powered programs in favor of teams made up of regular students. But they might as well let the stadiums rot. It's cheaper that way than to pay out of general univsity funds the enormous upkeep for the athletic plant while the ticket sales are used to pay the coaches, the equipment, the travel--and the recruiting costs."

"The universities try to tell the public that the athletic departments are self-sustaining but they are only juggling the books. Just examine the acounts in your athletic departments-- if you are allowed to--and find how much comes out of tuition, gifts, and state aid."

Temple said that his position makes him the "most-hated sports editor in the nation." "Coaches hate me, university presidents are embarrassed by me, and the fans detest me for blowing the whistle on their little games. Their is just one good thing about it: people enjoy hating me so much they read my column first in the paper."

38.

pain

Recent tests have upset myths about the ability of human beings to withstand pain.

The testing, however, was done on reasonably healthy people and did not give reactions of sick people to pain.

The results of the research was given today in Dallas by Stanford psychiatrist Dr. Kenneth M. Woodrow at a meeting of the American Psychiatric Association.

Dr. Woodrow, *of Stanford University* said that his study of 41,000 Californians showed that

1--men can tolerate much more pain than women.

2--Young people can stand pain better than older people.

3--Whites have a higher pain tolerance than blacks.

4--Orientals have the lowest tolerance of all.

The pain test was arranged by having a machine squeeze a person's achilles heel. The machine tightened the grip until the subject could not stand it.

Women could bear only half as much pain as men and some men could tolerate as much pressure as the machine could produce. Both men and women showed a decrease in tolerance as they got older. Men over 60 could take less than three quarters of the pain accepte by men in there twenties.

Dr. Woodro said that racial differances were far less clear. He thought that the pain experienced by some minorities was worse for them because it was being applied by white testers.

The purpose of the research was to assist doctors whose patients are in pain. Doctors realize that worry about a serious illness can make a patient much less tolerant of pain.

"We simply don't know, Dr. Woodrow siad, "if artifically applied pain is emotionally comparable to the pain of illness.

He said, howeve, that his findings could help doctors in determining doses of pain-killers to match the needs of individual patients.

39.

Nieman

Cambridge, Mass.--Twelve American journalist have been appointed to next year's class of Nieman Fellosw to study at Harvard University. The programme was established under the will of Anges Wahl Nieman in memory of her busband Lucius w. Nieman, found of the Milwaukie Journal.

The University has also appointed three Associate Fellows from Korea, the Philipines, and South Africa.

James P. Thomson, a Harvard University history professor who once was a journalist, has been names curator of the Fellowships. He succeeds Dwight Sargent, who is returning to newspaper work.

Stories that Skirt Libel

Stories in the rest of the workbook may bring a libel suit unless carefully edited.

40.

trail

Jason Richards, 24, who robbed a liqour store of $1,800 three months ago, will go on trial today before Judge Felix J. Schiding.

A jury is expected to be picked this morning and Asst. Dist. Attorney Roger Addams plans to call his first witness this afternoon.

Richards is accused of entering the Nadir Liqour Store, 714 W. Green Street, a few minutes before the 11 p. m. closing time on the night of Feb 15. He held a gun on Clerk Fred Myers and demanded that Myers give him all the money. *Myers did.*

Addams asid he would produce three witnesses: Myers, *two* A passerby, and Police Sgt. Wilmer Schnepp, who ran headon into Richards as he fled down the alley behind the store. Schnepp was knocked down but got up, chased Richards for three blocks, and made the arrest.

Richards is being defended by Attorney Walter B. Hubley. He is accused of armed robbery and taking $224.

~~The Nadir kig~~

The nadir ~~ta~~ Liquor Store has been robbed three times in the last two years. The Richards' haul is the most ever taken.

41.

lottery   By Tom Laue

Is it a painless way to boost state revenue or an immoral

sanction of gambling?

These are the main questions which have raged for years

over a state lottery. The State Assembly entered the fray

yesterday when it passed 99-63, a state lottery bill. Its

sponsor called it a "happy piece of legislation" that should

bring at least $100 million to the state treasury if passed

by the Senate and signed by the governor.

Rep. Carlo J. Giannini, (D-Rockford), said his bill would

yield revenue for the state that now goes into illegal policy

rackets and other n-mber games.

"This is a happy piece of legislation that will solve

the states' financial problems," he added.

The bill would give 50 per cent of the net proceeds--the

money left over after prize money is awarded and administrative

expenses have geen covered--to the cities on a per head basis.

Objection to the bill came largely in the form of fear

that the state would be endorsing immorality if the lottery

became law.

"I'm not so sure this si a happy bill," said Rep. Quentin Norris,

(R-Petaluma), "A great many people without the financial

wherwithal would be most attracted to a lottery. The people

losing will be the least able to afford it.

Giannini aruged figures from some other states with a lottery--there are six--show roughly half those taking part earn $10,000 a year. He did not say what the other half earn.

Rep. Brian O'Malley, (R-Sumton), tried to show lotteries can produce apathy and indifference.

"The first reaction of a Massachusetts lottery winner when he heard he'd get $50,000 for 18 years was, "I'm going to quit by job," O'Malley said.

The House reacted by chefring and hooting histerically.

Re. Peter Flaherty (D-Rock Falls) who last year steered a bingo game to legality and who now is trying to legalize raffles and chances, called lotteries "a painless and voluntary extarction of money for the state. I urge you fellows to get your marbles together and support this.
This charade of morality is no longer pertinent to the people of this stage. They work hard and pay a lot of taxes and they want this kind of lottery.

The bill would set up a five-member state lottery commission to regulate the lottery and the commission would be appointed by the Governor.

Gov. Sanford J. Walpole has not said whether he would support or veto the measure.

42.

cop

    Police Sgt. William H. Staunton, accused of accpting

protection money from a west side vice figures, was held

for action yesterday by the grand jury.

    He was released on a total of $1,000 in bail by Circuit

Judge Ethan Lincoln, before whom he had appeared for a per-

liminary hearing.

    Chief witness against Staunton was a former policeman,

Carl Staudenson, 27, and admitted former drug addict, It was

was his sworn statement last year that led to an investigation

into corruption by the police by the grand jury and by the

district attorney.

    Staudenson had listed seven policemen as being invovled

in corruption.

    Staudenson testified yesterday at the preliminary hearing

that he had received money for himself and for distribution

to other cops "for the purpose of refraining from arresting

known vice characters".

    He said the money, amounting to $4,000 over two years,

was given to him by Gerald Duffelmeyer, 46, 2349 W. Sycamore

Street. Duffelmeyer was indicted last week by the grand jury

for bribery, extotrion and attempt to solict corruption.

                                        or not
    Judge Lincoln will decide later today whether‸to set a

trial x date

43.

tech

By James W. Blair

Of Our Washington Bureau

Washington--The Caregie Commission on Higher Education recommended today that the federal government spend at least $100 million a year to develop electronic methods of teaching.

The Commission noted that it expected that viedotape cassettes, cable television and computers will be in wide use on college campuses by the end of the century.

The electronic devices can, in the long run, cut educational costs, provide more flexibility in teaching and provide more variety, the Commission said.

Dr. Clark Kerr, chairman of the commission, explained that cassetts will let people play recorded television productions of the classics in their homes or in the classroon. "It's got enormous possibilities," he said, "Just think, all the plays of Shakespeare at your library. I can hardly wait."

The Commission said that electronic teaching aids will provide the fourth revolution in education. The other three, the report said, were the shift from the home to the school, the adoption of the written word as an instructional tool, and the invention of printing.

The latest revolutin, however, seems to be faltering,
the Commission expounded. "The high cost of electronic equip- initial
ment the generally poor quality of "software", or materials
now available for use with the equipment, and faculty resistance hold back developments," the Commission said.

The Commission urged the establishement of seven regional
centers around the country to develop and di desseminate
materiels and techniques fro the new media. It recommended
bueilding a center every three years in such places as Atlanta,
Boston, Chicago, Denver, Houston, Philadelphia and San Francisco.

The federal goverment, under the plan, would finance the
cost of each center and pay for part of the annual expenses of
running the centers. The remainder of the operating budgets
would be paid for by colleges and universities making use of
the system.

44.

fish

Boulder City, Nev.-(A)-The Department of the Interior plans to build an artificial pool to save the rare desert pupfish from extinction.

The tiny pupfish found only in the warm waters of Devil's Hole in Death Valley, California, are in danger of extinction because of a lowring water table there.

Commissioner of Reclaimation Ellis L. Armstrong said the slightest drop in the water level could wipe out the pupfish because scientists believe the fish reproduce on a shelf only a few inches below the present water surface.

The pool, made of concrete, will be near the Colorado River on the Nevada side of Hoover Dam, he announced, with a nearby warm spring providing the fluid.

45.

guerilla

The lessons of Viet Nam will not be lost on potential guerilla leaders in do ens of area of the world, a specialist in South East Asia said in a speech last night.

"Rebels all over the world will notethe way guerillas fought off the established forcs in Viet Nam and then fought the mighty United States to a virtual standstill," Dr. Hubert K. Kelley told the annual dinner of the League of Woman Voters. Dr. Kelley teaches Asian history at the University of Minnesota in ~~Minneapolis.~~ *St. Paul*

"The success of the guerillas in Southeast Asia may well birng a series of uprisings. The forced withdrawl of American troops from Vietnam will also take American leaders very reluctant to get into any such action in the future--and rebel leaders must know this."

Dr. Kelley was introduced by Dr. Suzanne Rasmussen, chairan of the history department of Oliver College. The dinner held in Hotel Monroe, was attended by 175 people.

46.

rate increase

The City Bus Company has asked the state Public Service
Commission for permission to raise rates by 15 per cent.

If approved, the rates will go from 40 to 45 cents for
in-city fares and for fares in suburban areas within a mile
of city limits. Rates for routes that go to outlying villages
will go from 60 to 70 cents.

Tokens will be 10 for $4.00 for the 45 cent rides ~~$5,000~~
or $6.00 for the more expensive fares.

Ronald T. Farr, general manager of the company, said his
firm's profit margin has shrunk to 3.3 per cent and that "there
is no alternative to a far increase if we are going to stay in
business." He added that the company had done all it could do to
reduce expenses but that revenue did not rise as fast as
expenses.

Farr criticized City Council for building more city
parking lots. "They build these expensive lots and then rent
spaces for 25 cents a day. No wonder peopole won't ride the
bus when they can park all day for a quarter." He proposed
that all-day rates be made a minimum fo 50 cents.

Mayor Karl ~~Karl~~ Zeisske said that a few lots, several
blocks from downtown, rent spaces for 25 cents a day but most
of them are at least 50 cents and those in the heart of the
city cost $1 a day.

47.

hamlet
                              By Daniel Anthony

Wilma Larson played the title role in "Hamlet last night
in Civic Theater but most of the audience wished she hadn't.

The fact that a woman was playing Hamlet did not seem
to bother the audience after the first few scenes but her
acting throughout the night was stiff and routine. Some
of her words were slurred and it appeared that if she had not
spent the later afternoon at The Pub she would have been able
to perform better.

The applause that greeted Miss Larson when she first
came on tate was substantial but at the curtain call there
was only a flutter of handclapping.

The rest of the cast managed to salvage the production.
Homer DiCarlo was splendidly pompous as Polonius. Gladys
Williams was a first-rate Ophelia, and the excellence of her
acting made a decisive contrast to the work done by Miss Larson.

The sets on stage were magnificent. It is a trigute to
the production company that it can set up elaberate sets like
these for one-night performances. The castle scenes could be
presented by a mere partial turn of the castle. The changes
usually were done without closing the curtain.

The performance opened the theatrical season at The
Civic Theater. The next play will be Shaw's Man and Superman
and will be shown November 14.

congress

Washington (UPI)-A citizens group says about one third
of the House's 433 members are involved in businesses and
law firms that could be potentel conflicts of interest with
their legislative dutieies.

The group called the National Committe for an Effective
Congress (NCEC) said because of poor information about the
House's members and virtually useless information about
senators there were indications that the percentage is even
higher.

NCEC said the Congressman with outside interests should
end them, noting that two thirs of the "members apparantly
have found no inconvience or harship in refraning from such
outside activities."

NCEC said that last year 16 comgressmen withdrew from
the practice of law.

NCEC offered the following as examples of potenial
conflicts of interest positions:

--53 participate in the practice of law, either maintaining
an office or holding a partnershipf, or "some looser association."

--41 receive income as directors, chairman or officers
or otherwise serving banks and savings and loan associations
subject to government regulation.

23 have relationships with insurance companys, mutuel funds and real estate firms.

--65 have "close afiliations" in oil development, advertising and broadcasting media, farming "and a variety of industrial enterprises.

Several members were involved in more than one catagory.

NCEC said that its findings were based on financial disclosures for 1971 filed by congressmen with House Ethics Committee, It said that better information could have been compiled if the House required full disclosure of financial interests by members.

It added that it could not satisfactorialy analyze information filed about Senators.

49.

viet

Washington (AP) The U. S. told France 25 years ago that Vietnam was playing into communist hands and urged Paris to be "most Generoud" in seeking an early solution.

This information was disclosed Tuesday when the State Department removed the secresy label from another batch of offical documents.

The advice came after a proported cease-fire offer from Vietnum Communist leader Ho Dhi Minh. The offer was reported to have been transmitted by Veitnamese messenger bearing a letter of invitation from French Overseas Minister Marius Moutet to meet with Ho.Chi Minh. The messenger disapeared under unexplained circamstances. The French said the letter from Minh was never recieved.

Then Secretary of State George C. Marshal told the French "We fear continuation of the conflict may jepardize the position of all Western Democratic powers in Southern Asia.

50.

hospital

Hundreds of hosptial workers, members of Local 342 of the Drug and Hospital Union, converged on city hall this morning for a rally to prove that nurse's aides and medical technicians hols "some of the most important jobs in the world."

The rally also was aimed at pushing for quicker act. 'n in settleing the contract dispute between the workers on on hand and the city administration and private hospital operatrs on the other.

The demonstration was held in defiance of a temporary court order issued Monday. This order restrining the union from a work stoppage that absented an estimated total of 2,000 workers from their jobs for up to three hours.

Surveys of the hospitals indicated that though the walkouts were extensive they were not disruptive. None of the two city and three private hospitals indicated in statements released to the press that any of their services which are essential were denied.

Wilbut Morgan, president of the League of Voluntary Hospitals, with whom the union is deadlocked in a dispute over contract negotiations, said the league would "move forward as quickly as it can" on filing for a contempt of court citation by a judge.

Morgan is handling negotiations for city hospitals, too.

In the contract argument each side says the other has
disclosed a failure to bargain. The hospital league has made
an offer that would elevate pay by $6 a week. The present
pay is at least $130 a week.

The Union has asked for 15 per cent increase or $25 more a
week. They will take the higher figure.

51.

sewage

Richmond, Virginia AP The State Water Control Board
voted today to bring proceedings of criminal action against
the Hampton Roads Sanitation District for pumping raw sewage
three nights last month into Hampston Roads.

Sewage that was untreated and totaling more than
300,000 gallons was pumped into the harbor waters May 13,
14, and 15after one of the three "digesters" at the district's
treetment plant had malfunctioned.

The pumping did not get eliminated until water control
board oficials visited the plant at Newport News that night
of May 15. They had been alerted by one of their members
and ordered it discontinued.

Assst. Attorney Gen. Gerald L. Baililes said that the
sanitation district could face one charge for each night if
prosecuted for the dumpings. Conviction on each of the
charges could bring a fine that would range as low as $100
and as high as $5,000.

52.

steal

Jacques Klinedinst, twenty four, of 1314 West Forty-Forth Street, was arrested today on a charge is stealing all four wheels from a car in a garage at the home of Homer Norton, 1314 West Forty-second Street.

He had used a jack, stolen from a commercial garage, to elevate the car, and took the wheels to the same garage in an attempt to sell them.

Garage workers stalled him while they called police because they were suspicious.

Police said they would arraign Klinedinst before Associate Judge Elmer Crabtree later this afternoon.

Some wire service copy still appears in all-capital letters, or "all-caps." The editor should flick his pencil once under the letters that are to remain capitalized.

Paste this story and the following one together to make one story for a late afternoon edition.

53.

A123 STOX

New York (UPI)—STOCKS IN THE NEW YORK STOCK EXCHANGES RALLIED BRISKLY BY NOON TODAY.

ADVANCES OUTNUMBERED DECLINES BY A WIDE MARGIN AND MANY ISSUES WERE UP A POINT OR MORE.

AT 12 O'CLOCK THE DOW JONES AVEREGE OF 30 LEADING INDUSTRIALS WAS UP 8.28 to TO 946.57.

STANDARD AND POOR'S GENERAL AVERAGE OF 500 ATOCKS WERE UP 0.81, INDUSTRIALS 0.95 AND RAILS 0.60.

TRADING ON THE BIG BOARD WAS ACTIVE AND TICKERS RAN BEHIND FLOOR TRANSACTIONS AT THE OPENING OF THE DAY'S TRADING ON THE FLOOR.

ANALYSTS OF STOCK TRADING SAID THE RALLY WAS TRIGGERED BY A REPORT THAT FRANCE AND THE SOVIET UNION WERE GIVING CONSIDER-ATION OF A PLAN TO TRY TO ACT AS PEACMAKERS IN THE MIDDLE EAST.

SEVERAL OBSERVERS TOLD REPORTERS IN CORRIDOR CONVERSATIONS THAT THE PEACE RALLY X COULD BE BLOWN AWAY HARRIDLY UNLESS SOMETHING TAGNIBLE DEVELOPES DEVELOPES IN THE NEXT FEW DAYS. ONE OBSERVER TOLD ONE OF THE REPORTERS THAT, "HOPE MAKES A GOOD BREAKFAST, BUT A POOR DINNER."

ON THE AMERICAN ECONOMIC FRONT, THE GOVERNMENT REPORTED
THAT THE UNITED STATES PAYMENTS DEFICIT BECAME WORSE IN THE
FIRST QUARTER OF THE YEAR, OFFICIALS SAID.

54.

A201 STOX

2ND LEAD

NEW YORK (UPI)-A GLIMMER OF HOPE FOR PEACE IN THE MIDDLE
EAST CAUSED THE NEW YORK STOCK EXCHANGES TO RALLY THROUGHOUT
THE DAY TODAY.

MANY ISSUES ~~XXXXX~~ STARTED OUT WITH MILD GAINS AND BY
CLOSING TIME THEY WERE UP AS MUCH AS TWO POINTS.

THE DOW*JONES AVEREGE OF THIRTY LEADING INSUTRIALS WAS
UP 9.45 to ~~₤~~ 946.74.

STANDARD AND POORS' GENERAL AVERAGE OF ~~500~~ 500 STOCKS WERE
UP ~~0.97~~ 0.97, INDUSTRIALS ~~xxx~~ 1.02 AND RAILS 0.72.

TRADING ON THE BIG BOARD WAS ACTIVE ALL DAY LONG AND
TICKERS RAN BEHIND FLOOR TRANSACTIONS BY AS MUCH AS TEN
MINUTES THROUGHOUT THE TRADING DAY.

PICK UP A123 6th Graf X X X ANAYLSTS.

55.

A014

amnesia

KEY WEST, FLORIDA, JUNE 13 UPI A HUNDRED MOTHERS WITH MISSING SONS HAVE CALLED POLICE HERE ABOUT A BOY WHO TOLD POLICE HE CAN'T REMEMBER HIS NAME OR ANYTHING ABOUT HIS PAST.

THE BLUE EYED YOUTH, WHO APPEARS TO BE ABOUT SEVENTEEN, SAT IN THE POLICE STATON AND SAID "I'D SURE LIKE TO KNOW WHO I AM."

THE FELLOW SEEMED TO KNOW THE NEW YORK AND RHODE ISLAND AREA AND HAS A LONG SCAR ON HIS LEFT THUMB BUT THERE ARE FEW OTHER CLUES ABOUT HIS IDENTIFY. HE HAS NO WALLET WITH IDEN-TIFICATION, SAID SGT. EARL McCAIN, YESTERDAY.

"HE STOPS IN HERE AT THE POLICE STATION EVER ONCE IN A WHILE AND I TELL HIM ABOUT WOMEN THAT CALL. I ASK HIM IS YOUR NAME JOHN GREEN? AND HE JUST SETS THERE AND SAYS I JUST DON'T KNOW. MAYBE."

"HE PLAYS THE PIANO AND THE OREGAN VERY WELL AND HE IS
                                        TALL
160 POUNDS AND IS 5 FOOT 11 INCHES."

~~SERGEANT~~ SARGENT MCCAIN SAID THAT HIS OFFICE HAS RECIEVED MORE THAN 100 CALLS FROM AS MANY WOMEN, FROM AS FAR AWAY AS SEATTLE AND PORTLAND, ME, ALL CLAIMING THAT A BROADCAST DESCRIP-TION OF THE BOY INDICATED THAT HE WAS ~~HER~~ HER SON.

THE BOY IS STAYING AT THE SALVATION ARMY HEADQUARTERS WHILE IN KEY WEST.

56.

securities   From the Wall Street Journal

Washington-The Securities and Exchange Commission, as expected for weeks, tightened minimum net-capital requirements for operating broker-dealer business.

The SCE had proposed tougher rules for the broker-dealers last August and the changes they enacted paralell the proposed ones for the most part.

In issuing its rule changes, the Commission, which has long believed that existing capital standards are too weak, said the inadequancy of its former requiremants had been "well-demonstrated" in recent years by the financial losses of customers whose broker-dealers had financial difficulty.

Under the proposed rule changes, which primarily effect over-the counter securities firms, those wanting to get into the business will need $25,000, five times as much capital as current rules reuqire, and they will have to maintain that level throughout their functioning as broker businesmen.

Futhermore the agency imposed a strictor debt-capital ratio requirement during the initial 12 months of a broker-dealer's operations. The SEC rule change insists that a broker-dealer must not allow his debt to exceed eight times his net capital during the first year of operation. After the initial period the debt-capital ratio would ease to 20 to one, the current standard now

(Merge this story with no. 58.)

57.

A055DT

bomb

Detroit, Michigan ap A bomb exploded in the baggage
Comparment of an American Airlines DC10 shortly after takeoff
from Detroit's Metropolitan Airport on Monday night, *morning* forcing
the plane to make an emergency landing, the Wayne County
Sheriff's department said.

Eleven persons were reported injured. The plan ran off
the runway after making the emergency landing. The pilot
tried desprately to slow the plane down by weaving back and
forth on the runway,

At least eight persons, including two stewardesses, were
taken to Wane County General hospital but none of the injured
were believed to be seriously injured.

It was not known whether or not the injuries were suffered
in the blast, or when the plane--which had been bound for
Buffalo--ran off the leading north-south runway.

GT 0931 EST

58.

A124DT

second lead bomb

Detroit (AP)-A loose door on the baggage compartment of an American Airlines DC-10 shortly after take off her caused an explosion that first was thought to be caused by a bomb.

The door on the pressurized plane burst open soon *after* the plane left the runway. The pilot landed the plane, but with much difficulty and the craft went off the runway.

Eleven persons were reported injured.

pick up A053 third graf x x xat least.

GT 1034EST

59.

a287 Meningitis 330

by Leif Erickson
Associated Press Writer

SAN FRANCISCO AP - A new vaccine has produced a dramatic and spectacular drop in the number of miningitis cases that long has plagued Army basic training centers, and official of the Army Surgeon General's ofice announced Monday.

The routine vacination of all Army trainees, started last

October, has produced a drop in the ~~rate~~ rate of cases to
1 in 10,000 per annum, Lt. Col. Philip E. Winter of the ~~Army~~
Armys Surgeon general's office, said.

Only eleven cases and one death were reported in the
first six months ofthe vaccination program, Lt. Col. Winter
told the American Medical Association's proventative medicine
section. He said only one case developed in a vacinated GI,
compared with 124 cases and eight deaths last year.

Winter, a medical officer in the Surgon General's
disease control branch, said that in the past meningococcal
infections had peeked in the first three months of the year
at all basic training centers except Fort Ord, California.
At Fort Ord the problem spread th oughout most of the year.

In the first three months of the year--the first
quarter in which all trainees in eight centers were completly
imunized--the menigitis incidence has dropped to 0,14 cases
per 1,000 a year--about 1 in 10,000, he said.

Much copy from wire services is sent by teletypesetter (TTS), which permits automatic typesetting of stories. The next few stories are in TTS form.

60.

b010

Brown Recluse

OAKRIDGE, Ore. AP -
Roy Bounds, 28, a kingsize mil
lworker, was raking wood chips
at a shipping yard when it hap
pened.

"At first I thought it was just
a veneer splinter," he said,
"but later I discovered two
little fang marks and two tiny
drops of blood on the back of
my hand."

By the following day Bounds'
hand was swollen and the bite
marks had turned white.

A visit to his physician and
the 6 foot 5' 300 pound millwor
ker learned he had been bitten
by a small spider indentified
as a brown recluse, a cousin of
the black widow spider.

That was more than a year
ago and, after three rounds of
surgery, Bounds still is unable
to work or engage in outdoor
activitees. Hes beginning to
wonder if his hand will ever
heal.

"Evertime it looks like it's
healed, it just starts rotting out
again," he says.

Bounds, who was working at the
Pope & Talbot mill shipping
yard, was bitten by a spider
normally nativve to the south
central states of Arkansas,
Kansas, Missouri and Oklahoma.
The half inch long brown
recluse carries venom toxic to
humans.

Bounds' physician speculates
the spider came from an empty
rail car at the mill's shipping
yard.

A pamphlet prepared by the

U.S. Department of Health,
Education and Welfare says
that brown recluse bites are
rare, but for the occasional per
son who is bitten, "it is a
serious medical emergency."

  Bounds' whose hand is pro
tected by a heavy cast, has had
three skin grafts this year. An
other is scheduled this week.

————————

61. Ag

  WASHINGTON AP - An
Agriculture Department spokes
man says that rural develop
ment must advance on several
fronts at once if it is to suc
ceed.

  William Erwin, administrator
of the department's Rural De
velopment Service, says that
too often leaders in rural devel
opment are paralyzed by tough

decisions on which problem

the leaders should should give

top priority to.

"A community which needs

an industry for several reasons

finally decides that it needs a

water and sewer system in or

der to attract industry. But the

existing tax structure of the

community cannot afford the

system, even with federal as

sist_e_nce. So the community de

velopment is paralyzed," he

told a conference on nonmentro

politan planning.

"But a broad approach to de

velopment on several fronts si

multaneously must be em

ployed if we are to bypass such

roadblocks," he said.

62.

transit

Atlanta, Georgia AP Mayor
Sam Masell wants the U. S. Government to subsidize mass transit the way it has financed highways that have promotd use of
the automobile.

He wants the aid so Atlanta can
cut the bus fairs from 40 cents
to 15 cents.

Unless there is a federal sub-
sidie, he decalared, bus costs
will price themselves out of ex-
istence.

Masell said the federal government has spent billions on
the interstate system which
often contributed to people
shifting from bus transportation to cars.

This federal policy should
change, he said, and the tax
on gasoline that was insti-

Auted to finance the highway

program should, in prat, be

given to pay for mass city

transit.

63.

b256

   h lbylwyyfvyyx

 Racial Military 200

 WASHINGTON   AP - The

Pentagon's top civil rights offi

cer said Monday the racial situ

ation among U.S. troops in Ger

many had vastly improved

within the past year, but said

there is still cause for concern

by any person who is concerned

with providing equal treatment

for all Americans.

   Donald O. Miller said black

and other minority group GIs

still believe they are not ac

corded the same promotional

and assignment opportunities
as whites.

But, he said, they appear to
have adopted a wait and see at
titude to determine if the pol
icies instituted by Gen. Michael
Davison, the U.S. commander
in Europe, produce results and
not just "some great flowing
words of equality of opportun
ity."

Miller, who recently returned
from a meeting with senior
Army commanders in Germa
ny, praised Davison for taking
steps to insure that men placed
in confinement pending trial de
serve that form of treatment.

A major complaint of black
GIs has been that they were of
ten put in stockades to await
trial while whites charged with
the same offenses were allowed
to go free.

In still another area, Miller
said more blacks are being giv
en top commands. This, he
said, "provides tangible evi
dence to the soldier that there
is an interest and concern in
placing minorities in positions
of responsibility."

He noted that the Army's
first black division commander,
Lt. Gen. Fred Davison, has as
sumed command of the 8th In
fantry Division in Germany
three weeks ago.

64.

concert

The Minnesota Symphoney will open the city's winter
concert series in Abbott Auditorium on Nov 2, November) Desdemona
Carle announced today. She is chairman of the Series.

"We are fortunate in landing the Minnesota Symphony
Symphony, which is one of the nation's outstanding orchestras,
to open the series," she announced.

The six other concerts in the series have not yet been
arranged, she said.

65.

b295

Energy NL 300

By PEGGY SIMPSON

Associated Press Writer

WASHINGTON   AP   -   Sec
retary of Commerce Peter G.
Paterson said Monday That a
commitment to energy   re
search should match past ef
forts to land men on the moon
and to develop the atomic
bomb.

"I would predict that nothing
less than an Apollo, or to use
an earlier 'nuclear phrase,' a
Manhattan type commitment,
will be necessary to turn the
promise of energy research into
reality," Peterson said.

It will require stepped up ef
forts by both government and
industry, he said.

"While it may be very cost

ly adventure, it will also be a priceless one in terms of its meaning to our children," Pe terson told the National Coal Association.

He told the coal executives, "The key to your future as an industry -the key to our sur vival as a strong and viable society-will depend on how well we energize ourselves to mount a whole new scale of energy research,"

Today, Peterson said, the country spends about 75 billion annually on energy, but only about 1 per cent of that goes to research and development and most of that is focused on only one field, nuclear energy.

He said there must a be a prompt, thorough evaluation of what clean, new energy sources can be developed.

66.

smith

Washington—The Smithsonian Institution has put 10,000 more items on display but this time their millions of visitors can take home the exhibits.

The 124 year old institution will open a bookstore in the National Museum of History and tecnology tomorrow morning at 9 A. M. The store is an integral part of the Smithsonians complex of museums and galleries in the nation's capital, for it is devoted to the hisotry, life. people and places of the United States.

Designed to satisfy the studens of the most esoteric point of Americana, the store's list of topics range from ghost towns to chndlemaking.

67.

80a

Train

By LLOYD WILBURN
United Press International Staff Writer

Salem, ILL. (UPI)--10 persons were killed and approxi-
mately 150 were injured today when an Illinois Centrail Train
derailed near here. Damaged was estimated at more than
$500,000 by the railroad.

It was the worst railroad action in the nation in the
last deccade and the worst in Downstate Illinois history.
On Aug. 6, 1928, an IC train crashed near Mounds, (correct)
killing nine persons.

The dead today included men, women, and children. One
of those killed was the conducter of the train, Carol (correct) R. FLETCHER, 54, of 808 S. Locust Street, Champaign, *Illinois*,
a veteran of 36 years with the railroad. The anmes of the
other victums were not released.

The scene of the collission was Tonti, a hamlet 3 miles
northwest of Salem and about 13 miles northeast of Centrailia,
near where the railroad crosses Interstate Highway 57. The
train was traveling at 90 miles per hour, 10 m.p.h. under the
authorized speed for that area.

The train was the southbound City of New Orleans, which

left Chicago at 2 a.m. and was scheduled to arrive in New

Orleans at 7:30 p.m. The accident occured at 6:00 a.m., half

an hour after it had stopped in Effingham, Ill., WHERE three

persons deplaned. IIt is not knwon how many persons got on

or off at Champaign earlier, About 200 were abord when the

train left Chicago for Newœ Orleans.

"People were climbing out of the cars and lying mangled

on the rails and under the cars. Everybody was screaming.

Everybody was histerical."

So said Melvin Maxey, 63, a farmer, He and his son were

the first to arrive at the sene of the train accident. His

wife, Pansy, 60, arrive a few minutes later.

5-30 07:50 acd

82a

First ad Train 80axxxxxxxminutes later

The cause of the crash was not immediately determined.
Alan Boyd, president of IC flew to the scene in a chartered
plane. He was accompanied by other highranking officials
of the railroad, which is operating under the national ampex
A team of inspectors from the National Transportation Safety
Borad also were reported en route to the scene.

Their were unofficials reports that wheels on the lead
diesel had locked, but railroad officials reclined to comment.
The train included four locomotives and 14 passenger cars.
All units left the tracks. Seven cars were overturned.

The engineer, Lacy F. Haney, 902 W. Union St., Champaign,
was among the injured. He was reported in fair condition in
St. Mary's Hospital in Centralia and could not be questioned
by newsmen.

The injured were taken to hospitals in Salem, Centralia,
Mr. Vernon and St. Louis, which is 90 miles east of the accident
scene.

About 1,200 feet of track was twisted and torn by the
crash. Ambulances and fire equipment sped from nearby communities to fight the killing flames and rescue victims mangled
by the rails.

"God, it was horrible," one surviver said, "I saw a woman pinned under the rails, and she had to be cut free. She later

Another person said, "The cars were scattered like spaghetti.

An hour before the accident, passengers in car 13 had moved to car 14 when air conditioning failed in their coach. Among them was Mrs. Delores Raines of Kanakee, *Illinois* and her 15-month-old daughter, Lainia. They were going to Jackson, Miss., for Mrs. Raines' grandmother's funeral. "We just felt a little jerk," she said. "All I could see was rails, sticks and dust."

Car 14 stayed upright; car 13 overturned.

5-30 08:15 acd

89a

Second ad Train 80axxxxxxxoverturned

A 54-year old railrader broke down in tears as he re-
counted for newsmen the hrrror of the crash.

Kenneth H. Mays of Urbana, *all,* a 30-year employe of the IC,
who was not seriously injured, said he was at the rear of the
southbound train's third car, across a table from conductor
Carol L. Fletcher, when the accident occurred.

"I was sitting next to the wall when the train made a
little lunge," Fletcher said. "All of a sudden the north end
of the car went strainght up. Something popped the windows
out....my partner was thrown through the window...I would have
went out too if I hadn't been sitting next to the wall and
the window frame."

The Ic southbound tracks were expected to remain closed
until Wednesday evening as repair crews sought to remove the
wrecked cars from the scene. The accident happened near Tonti,
a hamlet 3 miles northwest of Salem and about 13 miles northeast of Centralia, near where the railroad crosses Interstate
Highway 57.

Alan Boyd, president of the IC, toured the wreckage for
an hou. He said the crossover switch was not opened and that
the track was in "first-class condition." prior to the wreck.

5-30 08:30 acd

68.

103a

Sub third graf 80a Train The deadxxxxxxxnot released.

One of those killed was the conducter of the train, Carol (correct) FLETCHER, 54, of 808 S. Locust Street, Champaign, a veteran of 36 years with the railroad.

Coronor Edward Perry of Marion County later released the names of eight other persons killed in the crash. They were Mrs. Vida B. Walker, 54, of Centralia, and the following from Chicago:

Mrs. Katheryn Adams, 35; her daughter, Gladys, 3; Mrs. Adams' neice, Natasha Smith, 12, who was traveling with I 's. Adams; Mrs. Toledo D. Samuel, 50; Geraldine Booker, 33, and Lynette Miller, 2, daughter of Mrs. Inez Miller, who was not injured.

Pickup fourth graf The scenexxxxxxxthat area.

69.

111a

second lead Train 80a

URGENT

By LLOYD WILBURN
United Press International Staff Writer

Salem, ILL. (UPI)--10 persons were killed and approxi-
mately 150 were injured early today when an Illinois-Central
train deariled after a roller-bearing failure caused a pair
of wheels on the lead locomotive to lock. The railraod
estimated daamge at more than $500,000.

Investigators fro the National Transportation Safety
Board, who revealed the cause of the derailment, said it
probably could have been averted if a warning light inside
the engine cab has been working.

Kirby G. Carriere, general superintendent of motive power
for the IC said the light had been rendered inoperative when
the locomotive was taken in for repairs, and a railroad employe
apparently forgot to restore it before the run to New Orelans.

"The locomotive had been taken in for repairs," said
Carriere, "and the light was rendered inoperative. It should
have been restored before the run to New Orelans, but one of
our men apparently forgot to do so," he added.

The train included four locomotives and 14 passenger cars. All units left the tracks; seven cars were overturned.

Pickup second graf It wasxxxxxxxpersons.

5-30 09:10 acd

70.

MAXEY

SALEM, ILL.--(Special)--Melvin Maxey, 63, a farmer had just finished breakfast and walked outside his house a mile from the railroad tracks when he heard the crash of the Illinois Central train this morning.

"My boy and I jumped in the old truck as soon as we called an ambulance," Maxey said.

"People were climbing out of the cars and lying mangled on the rails and under the cars. Everybody was screaming. Everybody was hysterical.

Maxey and his son were the first to arrive at the accident scene. Maxey's wife, Pansy, 60, arrived a few minutes later.

"I saw two little kids--about 4 and 6--who came running down the road crying their eyes out," she said.

"They wanted their mommy and their daddy. The last I saw of them was when the sherrif took them in a car and said he'd try to find thier mommy and daddy."

Maxey said he ran across a field to drirect the ambulances and fire trucks. "The engine was on fire, and flames were jumping 15 feet in the air," he added.

After the rescue work was under way, the Maxies returned home. Later, they went back and stood at the edge of a corn- field and watched workmen begin to claer the wreckage.

"It's a terrible thing," Maxey said.

Nearby, a woman's black, floppy-brimmed hat rested atop one of the steps leading into one of the twisted railroad cars. The neat lettering on the steps warned, "Watch your Step."

30

71.

d086

Sharing

WASHINGTON AP--With pressures mounting both for andagainst it, a $5.3-billion bill for federal funding of state and local government expenses faces a crucial test today in the House Rules Committee.

Propponents are asking for a rule shielding the measure from amendments and protecting it against a challenge based on its violation of House committee tradition.

If the committee grants such a rule and is sustained by the House, the bill will go to the floor Wednesday and be voted on probably Thursday.

But the Rules Committee is deeply divide.

If it opens the measure to amendment, Rep. Wilbur D. Mills (D-Ala.) may decline to bring it to a vote. Mills is chairmen of the House Ways and Means Committee which shaped the bill over minority opposition.

Dissident Ways and Means members and others want to offer amendments closing what they call tax loop holes.

On the eva of the Rules Committee showdown, Chairman George H. Mahon of the Appropriations Committee stepped up his attack with a "dear colleague" letter to all House Members.

Mahon objects to provisions which would stripe his commitete and others of their traditional power to approve or deny founds for various federal aid programs on a year-by-year basis.

The bill would set appropriations for five years, starting at $5.3 billion and increasing $300 million a year, for states and cities. This is a radicial departure from House rules specifying that other committees authorize payments, but only the Appropriations Committee can have the say on the money actually made available.

05-30-72 07.48acd

Notes

Notes

Notes

Notes